LEADER GUIDE

WARRIOR HOPE

Basic Training For Living On Mission

Bob Waldrep

Andrew Edwin Jenkins

WARRI**O**RS
MISSI**O**N

Crosswinds Foundation

For more information about content placed throughout the book, email info@CrosswindsFoundation.org.

Warrior Hope Leader Guide: Basic Training For Living On Mission

ISBN: 9798877897588

Thank you for being a leader and for facilitating a Center of Hope. The time you spend taking warriors through the *Warrior Hope* manual will prove invaluable to both those attending and to you as you learn to be on mission together.

Keep in mind that this course is not just for those who are experiencing or dealing with trauma but, just as importantly, **this course is also intended to provide a vehicle by which warriors might be on mission together helping other warriors and their families**.

This Leader Guide has been prepared specifically to assist you in maximizing your ability to help others navigate through the material and their time together in order to ensure each warrior has their best chance to receive the HOPE they need. Take time to familiarize yourself with each chapter and the accompanying PowerPoint presentation for that chapter prior to the weekly meeting.

It is extremely important that you read the "Before You Begin" recommendations that start on page 9. Here you will find a checklist with suggestions for what needs to be done prior to starting a Center of Hope. There is also a section which discusses how to use the Leader Guide— **a must read**.

It is our hope that this is just the first of many groups that you will be facilitating. We want you to know that we are here for you should you have any questions or need additional information of support. You can contact us by going to the Centers of Hope website at TheCentersOfHope.org.

Thanks again for being on mission to help those who have served!

CONTENTS

Getting Started

Before you Begin: Planning & Leading a Center of Hope   9

How to Use the Leader Guide   15

Meeting Checklist   19

Teaching Notes

The Introduction (A+B)   23

1. Mental Health   37

2. Emotional Health   55

3. Spiritual Health   69

4. Defining the Mission   83

5. Overcoming Obstacles   93

6. Partnering with Others   103

7. Facing the Past   113

8. Owning the Present   125

9. Embracing the Future   135

10. Facing Forward   143

About the Authors   153

GETTING STARTED

BEFORE YOU BEGIN: PLANNING & LEADING A CENTER OF HOPE

How to Determine When to Start

Pick / identify a start date. Keep in mind that, if you meet weekly, it will take eleven weeks to complete the basic manual— twelve if you decide to end with a celebration meeting in which the group comes back for a dinner and discussion about their experience with being part of the group.[1]

If possible, you will want to avoid periods which include a major holiday. For example, we recommend taking a holiday, such as Thanksgiving, and counting back twelve weeks before it to determine your group's start date. By doing this you will ensure that none of your meetings fall during Thanksgiving week. If you choose biweekly meetings you need to allow for at least five to six months for the meetings. Certainly there are exceptions in which meeting during a holiday might be good for the group (this might include groups tied to service organizations, such as homeless veterans). However, it's best to try to avoid this.

We have found that if starting the first groups of the year by early February we can complete three cycles of weekly groups per year. This considers not having any start between Thanksgiving and the first of the year.

Once you have set a start date there are certain time line goals you need to meet prior to the first meeting.

---

[1] A celebration dinner is a great opportunity to have participants invite other warriors to see what they have experienced and sign up for a future Center of Hope. It is also a good time to recruit graduates to become future COH leaders. See page 151.

Four to Six Weeks Out

Order the Facilitator Kit. If you got this Leader Guide by some means other than a Facilitators Kit, please order one now as it will include PowerPoint presentations for each session along with copies of the DVDs referred to throughout the *Warrior Hope* manual.

Order curriculum and DVDS. You will need to have the curriculum to distribute at the first meeting so be sure and place your order to allow enough time to get it to you. Make your best guess as to how many participants you will have and go ahead and place your order. If you intend to provide DVDs of the *Invisible Scars* and *Honoring the Code* films, make sure and order these at the same time as you place your manual order. As an option, both films are available for free streaming at WarriorsOnMission.org.

You can find ordering information for films and DVDs in the Facilitator section of the Center of Hope website. If you order the Facilitator Kit it will include manuals and DVDs, so be sure and deduct that number from the total you need to order.

Order signage. This is optional, however, it is recommended that you have signage that will identify your location as a Center of Hope. Banners for this purpose can be ordered from the Centers of Hope website. Please allow 2-4 weeks for delivery.

Start promoting and recruiting. Don't wait until the last minute to start promoting and recruiting. Ask other warriors to help you identify potential members. Remember, *this is not just for warriors who have PTSD and/or Moral Injury*, it is for any warrior who is seeking a new mission and/or wants to help other warriors in their recovery and healing.

(Refer to the Facilitator section of the Center of Hope website for swipe-text and graphics available for you to use.)

Secure a host / meeting location. When selecting a meeting place make sure it will be adequate for your group. Some places you may want to consider are: area businesses (particularly those that might carter to or have a veteran clientele), restaurants, service organizations such as a VFW or American Legion Post, churches, etc.— any place that will provide you the space and be supportive of what you are doing.

Recruit service providers. As the Basic Manual points out, it is important for veterans to connect with service providers – individuals, companies and organizations that provide specific services for veterans. We recommend you compile a list of such providers in your area to give to those attending. In the alternative, you might invite a representative of an organization to attend the meeting and allow them five minutes to tell about their service. If possible, have them stay around for the meeting and meet with any who want to talk further afterwards. You might also consider setting aside five minutes each week and letting members share information about a provider that has helped them or that they are familiar with.

Note: If you invite providers to speak at each meeting you must be willing to stop them at five minutes otherwise you will lose valuable training time with those present.

(The facilitator section on the Centers of Hope website contains tips on looking for service providers.)

Recruit Co-leaders or facilitators. Seek other warriors who will assist you. This is particularly necessary for large groups which will require such support leaders as greeters to be on location prior to start time, a crew who will make sure everything is set up and handle clean up afterwards (if needed), small group discussion leaders, etc.

Note: Each time you lead a group watch for those who you think will be good facilitators or co-leaders and helpers of the next generation of groups.

Make a decision about Challenge Coins. You do not have to order Challenge Coins right now but you do need to be considering if you will have a ceremony the last week and provide coins to those who complete the curriculum. You will need to order your coins no later than six weeks before your last meeting.

Make Sure to Have the Following at Each Meeting

Projector and laptop / computer. If not provided by the host location, secure a projector and laptop for using the PowerPoints accompanying each session.

Note: If you are unable to secure these items, the "How to Use the Leader Guide" section will address what to do if you do not have PowerPoint capabilities (pages 16-17).

Sign up forms. Make sure to have sign up sheets at each session to register new attendees. You can download sheets at the Centers of Hope website in the facilitator's section. It is important to have this information so you can stay in touch with your group with weekly email reminders of the meeting.

Note: please communicate to your participants that they receive free access to various videos and other training materials at TheCentersOfHope.org.

Additional manuals and DVDs. Be sure and have additional manuals on hand at each meeting, as you never know when someone new to the class will show up at the invitation of one of those attending. While a Center of Hope is based on structured material, **we NEVER turn away a warrior** who is looking for a place to connect.

Someone responsible for set up / take down. If you will be required to set up the room each week, recruit someone who will take responsibility for this so you can turn your attention to early arrivals.

Music. It is recommended you have music playing in the background as group members arrive. This helps set the stage for transitioning from what may have been a hectic day to a more relaxed time of being with fellow warriors.

Coffee and snack table. If possible, provide light snacks with coffee and, perhaps, water. Do not try to be elaborate— keep it simple— donuts, chips, or cookies, etc. If you have a host organization, see if they will supply these and include a sign on the table that identifies them as providing the snacks.

Name tags. Again, this is just a suggestion, but is particularly beneficial in a large group where it becomes more difficult to learn each other's names.

During the Meeting

The Leader's Guide goes into great detail to help you be successful in facilitating your groups. Following are a few reminders about conducting each meeting.

Arrive early / stay late. As the leader be sure that you and your team are on site at least thirty minutes before the start time to meet early arrivals. This also gives you time to coordinate set up and handle any last minute details that may need to be addressed. Also stick around afterwards in case anyone needs to talk with you.

Start on time / finish on time. If you wait for stragglers to arrive before starting, you will communicate to those who arrive on time that they can come later. It is important to resist the desire to wait for more people to arrive and just plow ahead with the discussion. If you do this you will find that the stragglers will begin getting there sooner.

In the same way, be respectful of members' time and end each session on time. This will take more planning on your part but it will be worth the effort. If you feel like there is something that yet needs to be covered or discussed, or if the conversation was getting lively, simply tell the group it is time to end but offer to stick around if any would like to remain behind and continue the discussion. This allows those who need to go the opportunity to do so and allows you to keep your commitment to always end on time.

Lead the discussion. When asking discussion questions recommended in this guide, don't be too quick to break the silence. At times you will ask a question that you know everyone will jump on and then you have fifteen seconds of silence— which seems like an eternity. Resist the urge to jump in and say something. Wait a bit longer and you may be surprised at the discussion that follows.

If you have a group in excess of twenty people you may want to limit discussion during the large group teaching and consider breaking into small groups of 8-10 after the main teaching time. This will require you to recruit small group leaders for each of these groups.

Note: find more information about leading small groups and managing COH of varying sizes in the facilitator section of our website.

When leading discussions, keep in mind that not everyone wants to share in public so don't call on anyone specifically unless you know they are comfortable sharing. If it appears someone looks like they have something to say, instead of asking them to share say something like, "Jim was there something that came to mind on this point you would like to share or are you just reflecting on it?"

Use the Meeting Checklist. On page 19 is a Meeting Checklist you can copy to make sure you are ready for each meeting.

Between Meetings

Review and look ahead. Take time to reflect on how the meeting went. Make notes of anything you may want to change or adapt. Also, note what went well and make sure to keep it in the program. Be sure and look over the material to be covered in the next lesson. Don't wait until you are about to walk in the meeting— plan ahead. The Leader Guide provides you with a detailed overview of each lesson. Take advantage of it when making your plans.

Email the group. Each week take time to communicate with the group by email. Remind them of the meeting and the topic that will be covered. Use this as an opportunity to also encourage them to work through the week's material to get the maximum benefit of the group time.

Meet personally. If there is someone in the group that you think needs a personal contact, try to arrange getting together for a meal or cup of coffee and talk.

Follow-up with your team. If you have others that are helping you with leadership duties be sure and follow up with them regularly to make sure you are all on the same page when it comes to responsibilities.

Contact service provider. If you have decided to invite service providers to speak at each meeting, contact the provider who is scheduled for the next meeting and make sure they still plan on being there. Remind them time is limited and to plan on having not more than five minutes. Invite them again to stay for the group meeting.

Order Challenge Coins. If you intend on giving your group Challenge Coins you need to order them no later than week four of the meetings. You can get ordering information at the Centers of Hope website.

*As you lead your group(s) go back and refer to this section often as you will probably pick up on new information as you get farther along in your group.

HOW TO USE THE LEADER GUIDE

Coming to Terms with the Technology

The Leader Guide is designed to walk you through each PowerPoint presentation. At the end of this section you will find information about how to lead the material if you do not have the PowerPoint presentations or do not have access to the equipment needed to use the PowerPoints. Be sure and read this section for, as wonderful as technology is, there will probably be times when the laptop, projector, or the human running them fails to work properly and you may find yourself without this helpful tool.

Each chapter in the Leader Guide begins with "Your Objective." This statement provides you the overarching goal for the session – what you want to communicate during the teaching time.

Hold your place here and look on page 23, where you will see the "Your Objective" statement. Below it, you will see a graphic which reads "WHAT IS A CENTER OF HOPE?" This is the first slide in the PowerPoint presentation and is also found in the Basic Manual at the top of page 9.

As you can see, the guide is laid out with each slide of the PowerPoint for the chapter located on the left side of the page. On the right side of the page you will find helpful comments to assist you in discussing each slide.

Note: You will find some slides are a graphic that is not found in the manual. In such cases the page number refers to where in the Basic Manual the concept or idea depicted can be found. Sometimes a page number is not given as the slide is simply a transition statement that is self-explanatory.

These comments on the right side of the page generally include:

- **Main Point**: A statement or overview of what this slide is communicating.

- **Page**: Identifies the page number in the Basic Manual where you can find the graphic upon which the slide is based, along with more information about that point.

- **Talking Points**: Pay particular attention to this section as it will usually contain the "must-cover" points and often contains questions to pose for discussion about the slide or concept being presented. Be sure and familiarize yourself with the talking points by reviewing the related information found on the page number(s) referenced from the Basic Manual.

  Note: for some slides you will only find a "Main Point." In such cases this is the "Talking Point" so additional commentary is not needed.

- **Quick Tips**: Throughout the Leader Guide you will find shadow boxes identified as a "Quick Tip." You can view an example on the bottom of page 24. These are for your eyes only. They contain information, questions, or ideas that will provide you additional understanding or insight about the point(s) being covered. Sometimes they will include "be sure to share" information and on others you decide if it would be helpful to incorporate it into your group discussion.

What if I Can't Access the PowerPoint?

If you don't have the PowerPoint Presentations or your laptop breaks down or won't connect to the projector, don't freak out, you can still effectively lead the session. Occasionally this happens to us so we designed the sessions so they could be led without using technology.

Rather than showing the slide ask members of the group to turn to the page in the *Warrior Hope* manual where the graphic on the slide can be found. Then read the slide and then cover the "Talking Points" just as you would if using a PowerPoint.

For example, turn to page 24 of the Leader Guide and note the first slide on the left hand side which is a quote:

> *"In my dreams I hear again the crash of guns, the rattle of musketry, the strange mournful mutter of the battlefield" (General Douglass MacArthur)*

Note the slide includes the page number of where it occurs in *Warrior Hope*– page 7. So, you would refer the group to page 7 and read this quote then cover the "Talking Points" or, in this case, the "Main Point" found on the right side of the page in your *Leader Guide*.

As noted in the previous section, some slides are not found in the book such as on the bottom of page 34 in the Leader Guide – "THE AGENDA." However, note that the "Main Point" does inform you that the concept on which the slide is based Is found on pages 21-22 of the *Warrior Hope* manual. When you encounter these slides you can refer the group to the pages it is based on or simply discuss the slide by reading the points in it to them. Remember, *slides not found in the book are the exception and not the rule.*

About video clips. The PowerPoints also include video clips. Of course, when you come to those you cannot refer them to a slide in the book. In some cases, you may have to skip the clip and simply describe its content using the talking points. If the clip describes a particular point addressed in the book you may also want to refer the group to that section for discussion.

Sometimes the clip is taken directly from quotes in the *Warrior Hope* book. This is particularly true of the clips of a warrior sharing his or her personal story which are at the end of each PowerPoint presentation. These stories are very much the same as those found at the end of the *Warrior Hope* chapter being discussed. For example, most of the video content for the clip of John McCarty at the end of the chapter 2 is found on page 59 of the Basic Manual. You may want to refer the group to that story and either read it or review it and talk about it.

*****

We highly recommend attending a Centers of Hope leadership conference to become a certified facilitator / leader as it provides you access to additional helps and resources. Visit the Centers of Hope website for more information.

MEETING CHECKLIST

Items to Bring to Every Meeting

☐ Workbooks for participants (bring extras on subsequent weeks in case new participants join)

☐ Leader manual

☐ PowerPoint slides / leader presentation

☐ Computer access (your own or one in the room you're using)

☐ Projector or television monitor if not provided (screen if wall space is not suitable)

☐ Audio (speakers for sound from videos)

☐ Cables and adapters— HDMI, audio, video, etc. (Verify you have what you need in advance. We suggest keeping a bag of your own adapters and cords with you, especially if meeting in a borrowed facility— even if the host location provides these.)

☐ Signup sheet to collect participants' names, email addresses, and best phone numbers (bring each week, so you can follow-up with new participants— be sure to email all participants during the week). Download the sheet we use at TheCentersOfHope.com.

Optional Items

☐ DVDs of *Invisible Scars* or *Honoring the Code* (a better / more efficient option is to refer people to the streaming site, TheCentersOfHope.com)

☐ Coffee / water / snacks

☐ Signage— Center of Hope banners

☐ Music (to play while participants arrive)

TEACHING NOTES

THE INTRODUCTION [A+B]

YOUR OBJECTIVE: PROVIDE PARTICIPANTS WITH A) AN OVERVIEW OF WHAT A CENTER OF HOPE IS, AS WELL AS B) HOW TO USE THE MANUAL.

Main point: The goal of this session is to connect with the warriors while outlining the expectations for the group. There are two sections to cover this week.

- Intro A explains what a Center of Hope is.

- Intro B explains how to use the manual.

Page: 9

Talking points:

- Let them know this week covers a lot of information, but future weeks will be interactive.

- Consider providing a light meal (pizza), as this lesson can easily be taught while people eat.

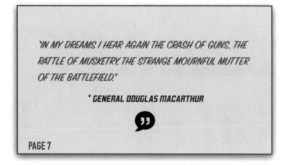

Main point: Show the quote to the left found on page 7 of their manual.

Talking points: Tell them there are many quotes throughout the book (most from warriors). Tell them to reflect on these when they come to them.

Main point: This ship is a great metaphor for Centers of Hope (COH). Namely, how different people might pilot the ship. Use the description in the manual to discuss how warriors options are similar to those available to ancient mariners in a storm.

Page: 9

Talking points:

• Most warriors have been trained to let others seek safety while they run into the storm.

• Point out for many the storm is inside of them and ask, *What do you do in that situation?*

> **Quick tip**: Since you are walking participants through this chapter, they may not go back and read it, so be sure you cover the main points. That way they'll know where to refer back if they have future questions. (Remember, this session is the first time that most— if not all— are seeing the workbook material.)

Main point: COH are the result of two feature-length documentaries Crosswinds produced. The first (*Invisible Scars*) dealt with PTSD; the second (*Honoring the Code*) covered Moral Injury.

Page: 10

Talking points:

- After watching the films, many people wanted a next step to discuss what they were learning. Centers of Hope is that next step. It is the actual progression these films— warriors sharing their stories and helping one another.

- The films are available free of charge to veterans and their families.

- We will refer to them throughout the manual.

Main point: Let's first outline what COH are

Page: Not in the manual

CENTERS OF HOPE ARE

* Regular meetings
* 60-minutes short, with the option to interact informally afterward
* Safe spaces to provide warriors with encouragement, resources, and relationships
* Hubs, where service businesses, service providers, & warriors come together to further the mission of hope & healing

PAGE 11

Main point: A description of COH

Page: 11

Talking points: The bullet points describe what participants can expect.

Remember: you can adapt time, place, and frequency of meetings to best fit your group. (Refer to the "Before You Begin" section.)

FOUR THINGS WE DO

REST	RECONNECT	RESUPPLY	REDEPLOY
FIND PEACE & HEALING	JOIN WITH OTHERS WHO CAN RELATE	OBTAIN RESOURCES WE NEED	MAKE MISSION ADJUSTMENTS

PAGE 12

Main point: These are important headings used throughout the manual and help warriors see where we are headed.

Page: 12

Talking points: Right now you are introducing the concepts. Some of this will make more sense for participants as they complete a few weeks of the curriculum. For now, just bring their attention to these.

Note: Centers of Hope is not about a building, a meeting place, or a meeting. It is about warriors connecting with warriors. It is not a program but a process in which warriors help one another find healing and a new mission.

Main point: After providing an overview of WHAT COH are, we move to discussing why we have them.

The next slide, a quote, will lead you straight to the talking point.

Page: Not in the workbook

"YOU'VE ALREADY FOUGHT ONE BATTLE, AND YOU ARE FIGHTING ANOTHER. YOU WON ONE ALREADY, SO WIN THIS ONE TOO. FIND A WEB AND GET IN IT, BECAUSE I DON'T WANT TO LOSE YOU."

† SGT. MAJ. JAMES JOYCE (RET.)

PAGE 8

Main point: This is one many quote slides shared throughout the book. Just read the quote and allow time to discuss.

Page: 8

Talking points:

Ask: *What do you think about this statement?*

One of the reasons COH exists is to not lose warriors— to not lose the battle.

Main point: Though this slide describes what a COH does, it's placed in the why section of this lesson, because one of the reasons WHY the Centers exist is to connect warriors to each other.

Page: 13

Talking points:

- The most important aspect of the COH is not the class— it is the warriors.

- The two-fold mission of COH is for warriors to find healing from the past, as well as define their next mission.

- The people in the group are important to one another—they are part of a web, a connecting point.

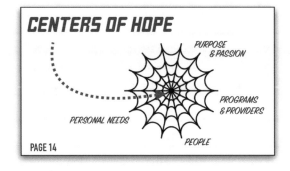

Main point: COH are the hub, the connecting point for many things.

Page: 14

Talking points: The four points around the web highlight a few of the benefits of the COH process, listed on page 14.

> **Quick tip**: Direct participants to the online materials. Though the online resources aren't meant to replace the group interaction, the online resources are a great supplement.

Main point: We place the info shared in the group, as well as the videos shared during the classes, in the Facebook group.

Page: None

Talking points: If you haven't already done so, pass a contact sheet and have people provide their email address, phone number, etc.

Main point: We've created a resource website where participants can review materials, find links to service providers, etc.

Page: None— this graphic appears throughout the book.

Talking points: Draw their attention to the online resources and encourage them to access the web portal- even during the class while you are talking.

> *'I TEND TO THINK THAT GROUP THERAPY IS PROBABLY THE MOST EFFECTIVE [TREATMENT FOR PTSD] FOR THIS REASON: IN GROUP THERAPY YOU ARE THERE WITH OTHER SERVICE MEMBERS WHO ARE EXPERIENCING SIMILAR SYMPTOMS, SIMILAR DISTRESSES, AND SO IT HELPS TO NORMALIZE WHAT THAT SERVICE MEMBER IS GOING THROUGH.'*
>
> PAGE 16

> *'AS A RESULT THEY WILL BE MORE LIKELY TO OPEN UP, TALK, AND TO SHARE INFORMATION AS FAR AS WHAT'S HELPFUL- WHAT THIS PERSON IS DOING THAT'S HELPED COMPARED TO WHAT THIS ONE IS DOING.'*
>
> * RAMSAY COUTTA, PHD, MILITARY CHAPLAIN
>
>
>
> PAGE 16

Main point: Back to the reason WHY we have the group. Groups are effective and efficient. They give people access to others who have struggled in similar ways- and overcome. And, they show we aren't alone.

Page: 16

Note: Two slides for this quote.

Talking points: If you have an illustration related to the value of a warrior connecting with others, share it.

This may be your own story or one you have heard about another warrior.

Quick tip: This is an information-heavy session. There isn't another one like it in the entire course. Don't apologize for the content- just keep the conversation moving forward, focusing on the benefits. Remind them there is much less material to cover in future weeks, so there will be far more time to share for those who want to do so.

Main point: Remind them that Intro A explained how the group works. Now you want to take a quick look at how the manual works.

Page: Not in the workbook

Talking points: This will lead us into the mechanics of the manual, Intro B.

If you have any late-comers, this is a great place to offer them a book.

Main point: Tell them to turn the page, detailing that Intro A outlined how the groups work and Intro B explains how the manual works.

Page: 19

TWO OBJECTIVES

1. FIND HEALING
2. FIND A MISSION

PAGE 19

Main point: The manual is written with a two-fold objective.

Page: 19

Talking points:

- Regarding objective 1, remind participants that even if they don't need healing (many will), they may know someone who does (which may be their mission— to help others find healing).

- Regarding objective 2, if they already have a mission, remind them they can help another warrior find theirs.

The info they learn will sometimes be for them— and sometimes to give to others.

Other: This is a great time to allow them to provide feedback.

See if anyone would like to share what they are thinking about the material discussed so far.

Quick tip: Don't pressure people to talk. When they are ready, they will speak.

If you know someone in the group who is willing to share, you may want to ask permission to call on them specifically— even before the group begins— for the first few weeks to "prime the pump," so to speak, as it may make others feel more comfortable sharing.

Main point: There are four units in the manual.

Page: 20

Talking points: The next four slides outline the different units. As you move through those slides, it's a great time to have them flip through the books, seeing what's there.

Note: If you are not using PowerPoint, the sub-points of each of these slides can be seen in the Table of Contents on page 5 of the Basic Manual.

Other: Notice that each slide walks you straight through the book.

- **Healing** = chapters 1-3

- **Opportunity** = chapters 4-6

- **Peace** = chapters 7-9

- **Empowerment** = chapter 10

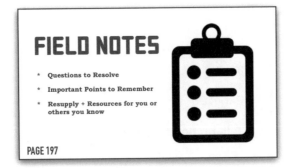

Main point: Refer the group to page 197 in the book and show them the Field Notes.

Page: 197 (Additional instructions are on page 198. Familiarize yourself with these.)

Talking points: Take a few minutes to show them there is a two-page spread for each lesson. This is space to write their thoughts, express ideas, etc.

Main point: Now that we've answered the WHAT, WHY, and HOW, we'll provide a few additional details to empower them to get the maximum benefit from the group.

Page: Not in the workbook

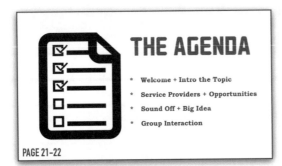

Main point: The introductory week is a bit different than future weeks. This slide shows them what to expect for the next 10 weeks.

Page: 21-22 (is not a graphic in their book— it's written as bullet points)

Note: Remind them that you will start and stop on-time.

Main point: Here's how to get the most from the group- work the material *outside* of the group time.

Page: 23

Talking points: Remind the group this week is an exception. From this point forward you will not be reading the book to them. Rather, you will cover the main ideas, and encourage them to wrestle with the material. They should read the book on their own- working ahead and reviewing each week.

Emphasize if they were unable to do the work, they should still come to the meeting as it will be of benefit.

Main point: Remind them again that online resources are available and encourage them to sign up.

Page: 24

Quick tip: Remember to start and stop on-time. The natural tendency is to want to "wait" when you have regular attenders who are not yet there— especially when you know they are on their way.

It is imperative that you begin on time and engage those who are present. If not, you will— without words— train everyone to arrive late.

1. MENTAL HEALTH

YOUR OBJECTIVE: REMOVE THE STIGMA ASSOCIATED WITH PTSD (AND MENTAL HEALTH IN GENERAL), SHOWING WARRIORS THAT INVISIBLE SCARS ARE COMMON, THAT THEY ARE A NATURAL RESPONSE TO WHAT THEY HAVE EXPERIENCED, AND THAT HELP IS AVAILABLE.

Main point: Title slide for the lesson.

Page: 27

Main point: The background is the image from *Invisible Scars*, a documentary about PTSD.

Page: Not in the workbook

Talking points: This a great opportunity to offer the film to participants and/or refer them to the COH website where they can stream it free.

Ask if any have had a chance to watch it. If so, ask for feedback from them, as this leads straight into the lesson.

Quick tip: After asking for input, take a pause, be quiet for a moment, and see if anyone answers— let people talk. You don't have to let the silence become awkward, but if you provide space many people will speak, taking the conversation further. If no one speaks up, then forge ahead.

'IF YOU'RE GOING THROUGH HELL, KEEP GOING. NEVER GIVE IN, NEVER GIVE IN, NEVER, NEVER, NEVER, NEVER–IN NOTHING, GREAT OR SMALL, LARGE OR PETTY–NEVER GIVE IN EXCEPT TO CONVICTIONS OF HONOR AND GOOD SENSE.'

* SIR WINSTON CHURCHILL

PAGE 26

Main point: A main idea to emphasize to people who are struggling.

Page: 26

Ask: *What do you think of this statement?*

Main point: Remind participants that we are in chapter 1 of the book, which is the first chapter of Unit 1 / Healing.

Page: Not in the workbook

Talking points: The name of the book, *Warrior Hope*, is based on this outline.

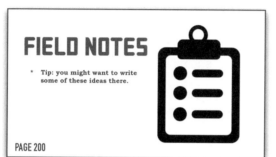

Main point: Read the main idea of the chapter.

Page: 27

Talking points: Give participants a chance to respond to what you read.

Ask if any can relate and would share something about their own invisible wounds.

Main point: Remind warriors that they have space in the back of the book to capture their thoughts as you teach.

Page: 200 is the location for the Field Notes for chapter 1.

Talking points: As noted below in the Leader's Guide, we refer to a few slides in this lesson that are not in their book. They may want to write your outline (the 5 main points).

Quick tip: This is one of the more complex chapters in the book to teach. Here are the 5 main points (note: participants do not have all of these slides in their books):

1. Perception can be reality (but it might not be, and some of it could be related to PTSD).

2. PTSD can be misperceived (we provide 3 misconceptions).

3. PTSD can cause misperceptions.

4. Misperceptions can cause denial.

5. Seek help.

1. Perception can be reality

1. Perception can be reality

YOU HEAR A SOUND AT NIGHT...

- OR -

CAT?   CAT BURGLAR?

Main point: Sometimes, our perceptions aren't accurate. Other times, they are.

Whether accurate or not, they help shape our impressions— how we see things.

Page: Participants do not have these slides, but the concept is taught on page 27 of the workbook.

Talking points:

- Ask, "What number is this?" (They should say "6.")

- Now ask, "Is it always a 6?"

- Then state, "It really depends on your vantage point, on your perception."

- From one person's vantage point the number is a 6. From the other, it's a 9.

- But it can't be both. Especially if the 6 is related to objective data— like how much money someone owes for a sandwich, how many days it is until payday, or how many klicks you have to march.

- The next example is common. You hear something outside and sit up in bed and think someone is breaking in- only to find out it was just a cat or dog. You move from a relaxed state to hyper-arousal (hopefully, it was just a cat!).

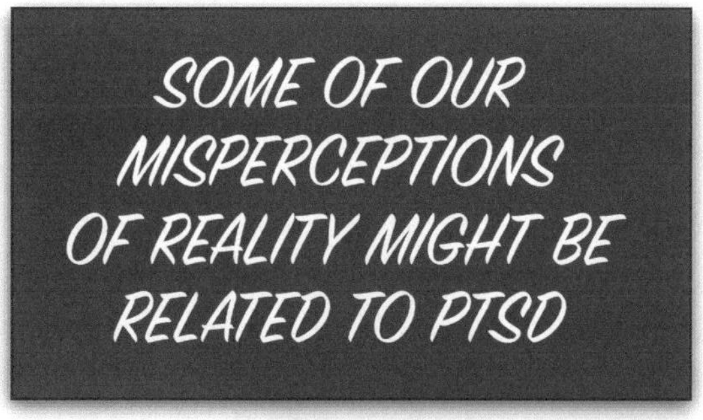
SOME OF OUR MISPERCEPTIONS OF REALITY MIGHT BE RELATED TO PTSD

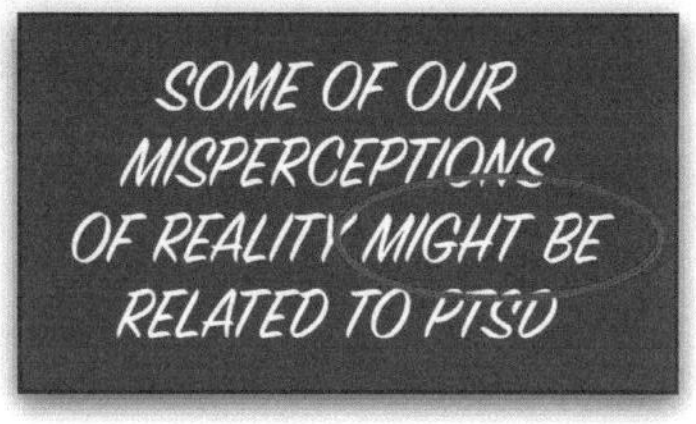
SOME OF OUR MISPERCEPTIONS OF REALITY MIGHT BE RELATED TO PTSD

Main point: Some of our misperceptions might be related to past trauma.

Pages: 28-29 (image not in workbook).

Talking points: Notice the emphasis in the second slide—the misperception might be related to past trauma. On the other hand, it might not be.

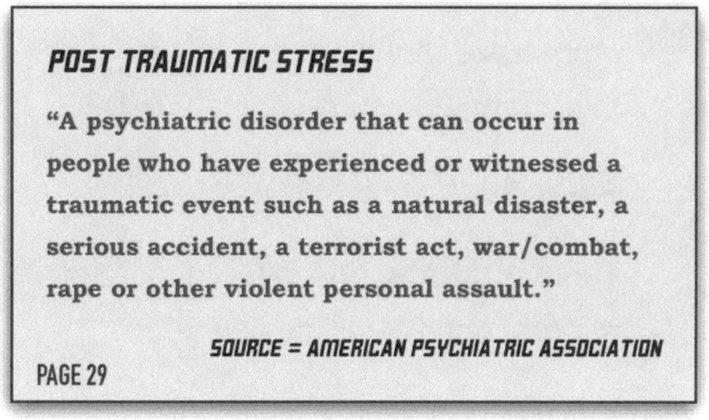
POST TRAUMATIC STRESS
"A psychiatric disorder that can occur in people who have experienced or witnessed a traumatic event such as a natural disaster, a serious accident, a terrorist act, war/combat, rape or other violent personal assault."
SOURCE = AMERICAN PSYCHIATRIC ASSOCIATION
PAGE 29

Main point: The official definition.

Page: 29

Talking points: There are a few points to raise:

- PTSD covers a wide range of experiences— not just war. Even for warriors, PTSD might not be related to a combat event.
- PTSD can occur if someone is the victim or even just a witness.
- PTSD is subjective to the individual. We all encounter the same experiences differently.
- At the bottom of page 29 in the Basic Manual we provide rationale for using the term "Disorder." For some, using this word is an issue. Please refer there for clarification you can share with the warriors.

> **Quick tip**: We are not trying to diagnose, treat, or prescribe. Nor or we attempting to evaluate how much trauma someone faced, or if military trauma is "greater" or "equal to" other experiences.
>
> Rather, we are opening the conversation and sharing ideas with warriors, so that they can identify potential issues and then seek help as needed.

2. PTSD can be misperceived

Main point: The second of five main points in this chapter. Here, we want to emphasize that there is a lot of misinformation surrounding PTSD.

Page: 29

Talking points: The following misconceptions will be covered:

- PTSD is new
- PTSD is rare
- PTSD is related to a physical injury

PTSD is new

MISPERCEPTION #1 OF 3

Main point: The first misperception (or myth) related to PTSD is that it's new. However, it's not new— it's been around a long, long time.

Page: 29

Main point: This is the first frame of a short video provided for you that recounts the history of PTSD— and how it's been know by different names throughout history.

Page: 29

Talking points: Look at the next slide, which provides a summary.

POST TRAUMATIC STRESS *IS NOT NEW!*

* Biblical times
* Civil War = "soldier's heart"
* WWI, WWII= "shell shock"
* Korea & Vietnam = "combat" or "battle" fatigue
* Today = Post Traumatic Stress Disorder

PAGE 29

Main point: PTSD has been known by different names throughout history.

Page: 29

Talking points:

· Participants may identify with these names, or even remember people from their past who were "labeled" in these ways.

· It wasn't until after Vietnam that experts began to take a serious look at the trauma experienced by Vietnam veterans and gave it the medical diagnosis Post Traumatic Stress Disorder.

Main point: The second misperception is that PTSD is rare.

Page: Not in the workbook.

Talking points: Notice the slide below.

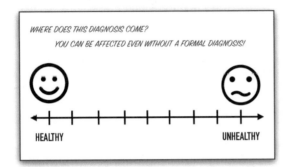

Main point: PTSD isn't rare. What's rare is the diagnosis. It's been estimated that 25-30% of warriors return home with PTSD.

Page: Not in the workbook.

Talking points: In order to receive a formal diagnosis with the VA, warriors must meet all eight criteria, as well as two additional specifications in the DSM.

- Many people don't meet all eight; they fall somewhere on the range between completely "healthy" and totally "unhealthy."

- This means most people will benefit from some degree of emotional help.

- Participants need to be honest with themselves, as outward appearances can be deceiving.

- In the next chapter, participants will take the PTSD self-check on pages 57-58 of their workbook.

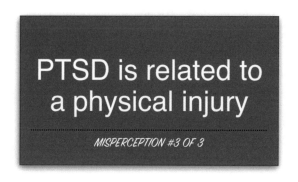

Main point: The third misperception we'll cover is that PTSD is always related to a physical injury. Turns out, it might be, but it might not be.

Page: Content on page 30.

Talking points: See next slide for talking points.

TRAUMATIC BRAIN INJURY VS. PTSD	TBI	PTSD
PHYSICAL INJURY	YES	POSSIBLY- PHYSICAL TRAUMA MAY ACCOMPANY THE MENTAL OR EMOTIONAL INJURY
MENTAL OR EMOTIONAL	POSSIBLY- EMOTIONAL TRAUMA MAY ACCOMPANY THE PHYSICAL INJURY	YES

PAGE 31

Main point: This slide highlights the differences between TBI & PTSD.

Page: 31

Talking points: TBI (Traumatic Brain Injury) is a physical issue; PTSD is a mental / emotional issue. They are different. They may accompany each other, but— as outlined in the book— they are two different issues.

Quick tip: Make sure you understand the difference between PTSD & TBI. Particularly note that PTSD may occur at the same time as a physical trauma event, but healing the physical trauma will not heal the PTSD. They are separate.

Remember, our goal isn't to diagnose (or avoid one, either). Our goal is health & wholeness—whatever path it takes to get there— and to encourage those who need help to get that help.

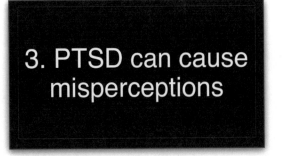

Main point: The third main point of the chapter is that PTSD often causes us to misperceive the world around us.

Page: None

Talking points: The next slide will lead into group discussion, as many warriors can relate to this.

Main point: Many warriors relate to experiencing something at home and instantly finding themselves emotionally / mentally taken back to deployment.

Page: None

Talking points: Ask if anyone can relate to this slide.

If you give them time, many participants may share a time when they've experienced this.

Quick tip: The following points are important. We don't want anyone to feel like they are "defective" because they have a mental or emotional problem. We've just discussed how our emotions can "transport us" to a different time and place. Now, we're about to make an important observation about that.

Many times, your behavior is consistent with your training and/or your past experience.

Your response would be completely appropriate in a different time + location.

Main point: These two slides flow together. The main idea is to show them that their behavior isn't "weird"— that they aren't flawed.

What's "off" is the location and timing of the response— not the reaction itself.

Page: Not in book.

Talking points: If you're in a combat arena and hear noise like gunfire, it's completely appropriate to drop and roll. However, if you're on Main Street, USA and a truck backfires, that response is not necessarily proper.

Stop and get their feedback. Those who can affirm these statements have taken an important step in the recovery process— acknowledging there is an issue.

"APOCALYPSE NOW"
ZOETROPE STUDIOS / UNITED ARTIST

Main point: This short film clip from *Honoring the Code* features Col. Mary Neal Vieten, who reminds soldiers that they aren't flawed. They're highly trained. What they feel is a normal response.

Page: Not in book.

We might mentally or emotionally react to a *different* event than the one we are experiencing.

(PERCEPTION CAN BE REALITY)

Main point: This slide helps summarize main idea #3, that PTSD can cause misperceptions.

Page: None

Talking points: In the previous example of the truck backfire, you hear the sound but you're responding to the memory of being under attack or to past conditioning.

4. Misperceptions cause denial

Main point: This leads us to the fourth main idea of this lesson. Because PTSD is misperceived (point 2) and because it creates misperceptions (point 3), we often deny that we're struggling.

Page: None

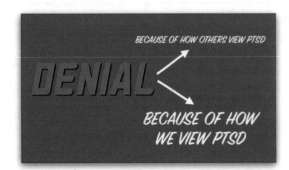

BECAUSE OF HOW OTHERS VIEW PTSD

DENIAL

BECAUSE OF HOW WE VIEW PTSD

Main point: Here, we highlight two reasons we deny wrestling with invisible scars.

Page: Not in book, but concept is discussed on page 31.

Talking points: Notice how this leads us to the quotes which follow— all from warriors.

> WHEN A SOLDIER COMES HOME, THEY DON'T WANT TO BE REFERRED TO MENTAL HEALTH, THEY JUST WANT TO GO HOME. THEY'RE OFTEN WORRIED ABOUT GETTING A JOB- SAY WITH LAW ENFORCEMENT. PEOPLE WORRY ABOUT SECURITY CLEARANCES- THE SO CALLED QUESTION 21 ABOUT WHETHER YOU'VE HAD MENTAL HEALTH TREATMENT.
>
> **⁺ DR. ELSPETH RITCHIE, RET. COL. [USA]**
>
>
>
> PAGE 32

Main point: A look at what veterans have said about the issue.

Pages: 32-33

Talking points: Read the quotes on these pages, which come from the two Crosswinds documentaries.

After reading the quotes, ask: *Can you relate to what any of these warriors are saying?*

Also ask, *Do you agree with their assessment— why or why not?*

> TO TALK ABOUT THE INVISIBLE SCARS IN MY DAY... WELL, YOU JUST FLAT OUT DIDN'T DO IT. YOU WERE A MAN, SO YOU "MANNED UP." YOU TOOK IT, AND YOU WENT ON.
>
> YOU KNOW THE CULTURE IN THE MILITARY IS THAT YOU DON'T GET SICK. IF YOU WENT TO THE SICK HALL THEY CALLED YOU A WUSS. "WHAT'S GOING ON?," EVERYONE ASKED...
>
> **⁺ JOHN MCCARTY, VIETNAM VET**
>
>
>
> PAGES 32

> ...SINCE YOU KNOW THAT ABOUT GETTING PHYSICALLY SICK, HOW MUCH HARDER, THEN, IS IT TO ADMIT SOMETHING EMOTIONALLY!?
>
> IN THE MILITARY, THE CULTURE WASN'T THERE FOR A MAN- OR EVEN A WOMAN- TO SAY, "HEY, THERE IS SOMETHING GOING ON HERE THAT I DON'T UNDERSTAND, I DON'T KNOW HOW TO RELATE."
>
> WE SAW IT, AND WE KNEW IT WAS HAPPENING, BUT WE JUST WENT PAST IT. YOU JUST GET OVER IT AND MOVE ON.
>
> **⁺ JOHN MCCARTY, VIETNAM VET**
>
>
>
> PAGES 32

> THAT ROUGH AND TOUGH TYPE OF ATTITUDE, YOU KNOW... THAT YOU'VE GOTTA BE THE TOUGHEST SOLDIER, THE STRONGEST LEADER, THE BEST OF THE BEST. YOU BELIEVE IT, SO YOU TRY TO TUNE OUT ANY WEAKNESS.
>
> IF YOU'RE DOING A SIX MILE RUN AND THEY KNOW YOU'RE CRAMPING, THEY SAY, "SUCK IT UP DRIVE ON SOLDIER!" SO THAT'S WHAT YOU DO. YOU DEAL WITH IT. AND WHEN YOU'RE TRAINING TO GO TO COMBAT, YOU DON'T GET TO TELL THE ENEMY, "HOLD ON MAN, I GOT A CRAMP!" IT'S NOT LIKE THAT.
>
> **⁺ JOE MONTALBAND, IRAQ WAR VETERAN**
>
>
>
> PAGE 32-33

THREE REASONS WHY

* STEREOTYPED CRAZY
* SIGN OF WEAKNESS
* TRAINED TO PUSH ON

PAGE 33

Main point: These are common stigmas associated with PTSD that cause warriors to avoid talking about it.

Page: 33

Talking points: Point out that warriors tend to think they should "fix it on their own." That's their training— and to do otherwise is to be weak.

Many participants will share their thoughts here, if given the opportunity.

5. Seek help

Main point: We want to encourage warriors to release the stigmas associated with mental health. This slide— and the next two— reinforce this idea.

Page: None.

Talking points: Notice the two slides which follow:

* First, we provide a few reminders about PTSD (It's real, it's common, and treatment works).

* Second, invisible scars aren't like physical ones— they aren't always so obvious. We might feel like something isn't quite right, but not be able to pinpoint it. And, it's hard to "own it" if you can't see it (or, if you feel like you need to hide it because of a stigma). Until we "own it" we won't seek treatment.

POST TRAUMATIC STRESS

* REAL
* COMMON
* TREATMENT WORKS

PHYSICAL ISSUES...

OBVIOUS = *CAN'T HIDE THEM*
OWNED = *ADMIT HAVING THEM*

You've rewired your brain before- as part of your training

PAGE 34

Main point: This brings us to one of the most important sub-points of the chapter, content specific about warrior training and the brain.

Page: Not in book. Content is covered on pages 34-37.

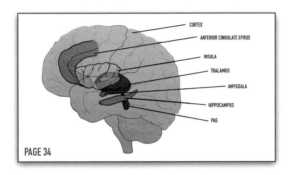

PAGE 34

CORTEX
ANTERIOR CINGULATE GYRUS
INSULA
THALAMUS
AMYGDALA
HIPPOCAMPUS
PAG

Main point: We want to emphasize how they brain works— normally.

Page: 36

Talking points: Most people flee from danger. It's a normal response.

Warriors, however, have been trained to ignore that natural response (a natural, primal instinct to protect one's self), logically think about what's happening, and then respond from their training as professionals.

This is certainly a positive trait and needed in combat, but it may also keep one from recognizing their trauma and seeking the help they need.

Quick tip: Spend some time reading pages 34-37 about how the brain works. You don't have to communicate the specific parts of the brain and every nuance of the neuro-chemical process. However, you do need to communicate that warriors are trained to do things that other people don't do— they see danger and then fight against it rather than fleeing from it. Their training enables them to overcome the natural "flight or fight" reaction to danger and, instead, act based on their skillset.

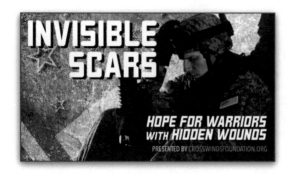

Main point: This is the cover of Invisible Scars, the documentary about PTSD.

Page: None

Talking points:

- This is a great resource for veterans who need language for what they have experienced.

- This is also a great resource for family members who want to understand a loved one.

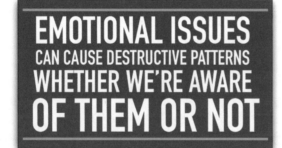

Main point: Emotions that get buried eventually surface in some way.

Page: None. This is a summary slide of the main ideas of this chapter.

Talking points: You may want to ask a few leading questions, such as where they have seen destructive patterns in others or even themselves.

Many times, addictions, relational issues, and even employment matters are the result of unseen wounds.

Main point: The final slide of this chapter is the first "Real People > Real Progress" video, featuring Patrick Breasseal.

Page: Matches the story on page 43.

Talking points: The videos always refer back to the main idea of the chapter, and typically open much dialogue. Leave some time for discussion.

2. EMOTIONAL HEALTH

YOUR OBJECTIVE: COMMUNICATE THAT ALL OF OUR EMOTIONS ARE HELPFUL. RATHER THAN "STUFFING" THEM, WE SHOULD LEARN TO HEAR WHAT OUR FEELINGS TELL US SO THAT WE CAN RESPOND— NOT REACT— IN HEALTHY WAYS.

EMOTIONAL HEALTH

CHAPTER 2

PAGE 47

Main point: Title slide for the lesson.

Page: 47

MAIN IDEA

2. EMOTIONAL HEALTH

THERE AREN'T GOOD EMOTIONS AND BAD EMOTIONS. ONLY HEALTHY AND UNHEALTHY EXPRESSIONS OF THEM. EMOTIONAL HEALTH IS A COMPONENT OF TOTAL HEALTH.

PAGE 47

Main point: Read the main idea

Page: 47

Talking points: Ask, *What do you think about this statement?*

Then, ask them if some emotions are perceived as good and some perceived as bad— and have them identify which ones are which.

(We're going to learn that even the so-called "bad" ones serve us and have a rightful place.)

1. SNAFUs should be the exception not the norm

Main point: We're used to SNAFUs occurring— hopefully as the exception.

Page: Slide not in workbook

Talking points: Ask warriors about SNAFUs they experienced while deployed. You may get some funny stories.

Ask if they've ever found themselves emotionally "SNAFU'ed." Hopefully, those times are exceptions. However, for many, they become the norm.

(Example: thinking it's normal to be let down, resulting in being stuck in a pity party of "Why try?")

Quick tip: There are four main points in this lesson. Here's the flow:

1. SNAFUs should be the exception not the norm.

2. Emotional health = part of total health.

3. Emotional health doesn't avoid tough thoughts or feelings.

4. We can read the signs of Post Traumatic Stress.

---

2. Emotional health = part of total health

Main point: The second main point of this lesson = get participants to see that emotional wholeness is part of their overall health.

Page: This slide is not in the workbook

* WHAT MAKES PEOPLE NERVOUS ABOUT DISCUSSING EMOTIONS...?

* WHAT MAKES PEOPLE NERVOUS ABOUT DISCUSSING EMOTIONS...?
  * STEREOTYPED AS CRAZY
  * THOUGHT TO BE WEAK
  * TRAINED TO PUSH THROUGH

* WHAT MAKES PEOPLE NERVOUS ABOUT DISCUSSING EMOTIONS...?
  * STEREOTYPED AS CRAZY
  * THOUGHT TO BE WEAK
  * TRAINED TO PUSH THROUGH

* COMPLETE THIS IDEA- I DON'T LIKE TO TALK ABOUT MY EMOTIONS, BECAUSE...

Main point: Open the discussion with the question on the slide.

If we can get participants discussing the fears they have related to emotions we will be in a better place to do the tough inner work of the soul.

*** Note: all three of these slides fit together, building on one another. After asking the question on the first slide and giving the warriors a chance to respond with their ideas, move to the next slide.**

Page: Look at page 45 of the workbook— at the end of chapter 1. We always include two questions at the conclusion to help people begin considering the next topic. This is one of the questions at the end of the previous chapter.

Remind participants the questions at the end of each chapter anticipate the content of the next lesson.

Talking points: Again, give the warriors time and space to talk.

Look back at page 33 of the workbook— the answers to this question are the very same reasons warriors give for not seeking help.

For example, someone says, "It makes me vulnerable."

Point out that this is simply not wanting to appear to be weak.

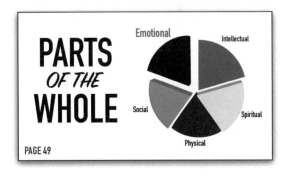

> "THERE IS A TIME FOR EVERYTHING, AND A SEASON FOR EVERY ACTIVITY UNDER THE HEAVENS... A TIME TO KILL AND A TIME TO HEAL, A TIME TO BREAK DOWN AND A TIME TO BUILD, A TIME TO WEEP AND A TIME TO LAUGH, A TIME TO MOURN AND A TIME TO DANCE."
>
> + KING SOLOMON
>
> PAGE 46

Main point: Notice that Solomon, who some say was the wisest man who ever lived, acknowledged that there was a time for both "good" emotions and "bad" emotions. Or, at least, the ones we often label as "good" and "bad."

Page: 46

PARTS OF THE WHOLE

Emotional
Intellectual
Social
Spiritual
Physical

PAGE 49

Main point: Show participants the bigger picture, that what happens in one area may affect every area— they can't be segmented.

Page: 49

Talking point: See the next slide for more clarification on this point.

Quick tip: Do not be surprised if some of the concepts you present to the group are new. Many people have been taught to "squash" or "bury" their feelings. Many people also consider emotions to be an ancillary part of us, rather than something that is essential to our personality and overall health.

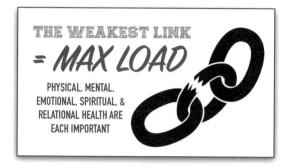

Main point: Since what happens in one area can affect other areas, our weakest area determines how healthy we can be.

Page: Slide not in workbook— this concept is discussed on page 49.

Talking points: Think about a chain:

- Each link is rated to hold a specific capacity. A chain with 999 links that can hold 1,000 pounds but 1 link that can only hold 100 will break once the weight reaches 100.

- In similar fashion, even if we're healthy physically and intellectually, our emotions can become our breaking point. In fact, any area can become the breaking point.

Main point: We commend people who hire physical trainers and people who seek treatment for physical illnesses.

Page: 53

Talking points: Ask warriors what people tend to immediately think when they learn someone is going to counseling. Or, what are the stereotypes?

? WHAT WOULD HAPPEN IF WE...?

* TOOK EMOTIONAL CAPACITY AS SERIOUS FINANCIAL CAPACITY?
* DEALT WITH EMOTIONAL HURTS LIKE WE DO PHYSICAL WOUNDS?
* ENCOURAGED EMOTIONAL GROWTH LIKE INTELLECTUAL GROWTH?
* EXPLORED WHAT'S HAPPENING INSIDE OF US...?

Main point: Get participants pondering the possibilities of what could happen…

Page: Slide not in workbook, but this topic is covered in the text on pages 48-49.

Talking points: Refer to the slide and ask, *What do you think would happen if we did these things?*

3. Emotional health doesn't avoid tough thoughts or feelings

Main point: Emotional wholeness doesn't mean we just "act happy" or deny the reality of hard things. Our emotions are given to us— as gifts— to interact with and explore the world around us.

Page: Not in workbook

Talking points: In the same way physical pain and pleasure are both good (think about what could happen if we didn't ever feel physical pain when we touched something hot, or when we broke a bone, etc.), so also is emotional joy and pain.

If time permits, allow the participants to discuss this concept.

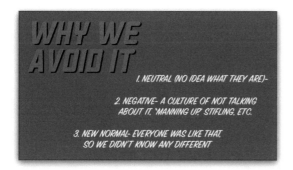

Main point: There are several reasons we avoid dealing with emotions— they range from neutral, to negative, to new normal.

Page: Slide is not in workbook— look at the bottom of page 51 for a list.

Talking points: Ask, *Do you think one of these is more common or likely than the other two?*

Note: There is not a right answer. You are just trying to get everyone to think about it.

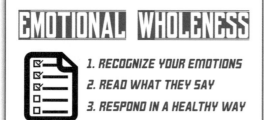

Main point: Again, our goal isn't to avoid tough emotions. Even those can communicate to us. But, rather than reacting in the moment, we want to respond intentionally— even if it means we must press pause for a bit.

Page: Not in workbook

Talking points: Ask participants if they've ever reacted in the wrong way — and later realized a better way they could have responded.

As a follow-up, *Would it have helped to have paused first and thought through your response?*

Though some may answer, this is a question they probably don't need to answer aloud. The goal is to get them to begin thinking about their responses before acting— not afterwards.

Quick tip: The concepts on these two slides are important. We want to move participants from "avoiding" emotions (i.e., as outlined in the first slide) to learning to recognize them (even the "bad" ones), reading what those feelings communicate, and then responding in a healthy way— even in tough or potentially volatile circumstances.

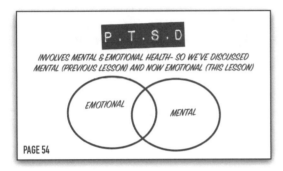

Main point: This slide shows us how PTSD involves our thinking and our feeling— both.

Page: 54

Talking points: Tell them to take note that PTSD is not just mental, but also emotional. Both must be addressed.

4. We can read the signs of Post Traumatic Stress

Main point: This slide leads us to the next video— an overview of PTSD.

Page: Not in workbook

Main point: This 60-second video, taken from Invisible Scars, provides a great overview of PTSD.

Note: if you don't have access to a projector, proceed to the next slide.

Main point: This slide reviews the previous video, highlighting the four common characteristics of PTSD.

Note that the result might be a fight or flight response. (Some participants may suggest that "freeze" is a third response, but it's more akin to flight—not facing it.)

Page: 55

Talking points: Ask warriors if they've experienced any of these feelings.

Remind them that warriors have been trained to face the threat and "fight," rather than giving in to the natural instinct to run. As a result, many may be hesitant to admit to these feelings.

Point out that some of the behaviors associated with PTSD may cause a warrior to feel embarrassed, or like a failure, thus compounding the problem.

> We've discussed the (valid) reasons why people don't want to deal with it, but the reasons to check yourself are greater.

Main point: Remember, earlier we discussed why people don't share emotions. Some of the reasons mentioned in the book were that others might believe they are crazy or weak— and that warriors have been trained to push through when things get tough.

Page: Not in workbook

Talking points: Ask, *Are the reasons for pursuing emotional health greater than the reasons for not doing so? Why or why not?*

- We *don't* want to invalidate a person's rationale for not wanting to get help. Face it, there are valid reasons, things that do happen (see point 2 of this chapter, Emotional Health = part of total health, on page 56 of this Leader Guide).

- We *do* want to emphasize that the reasons for getting help are radically greater than any of those reasons.

PAGE 57

Main point: This slide refers to the Self-Check included in the manual

Page: Slide not in workbook— the Self-Check is on pages 57-58.

Talking points: Ask if anyone has had a chance to review the assessment and would like to share what they've gleaned from it— not necessarily the results, but did they find it helpful.

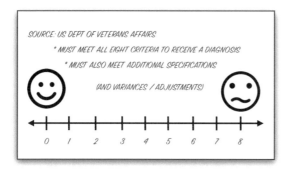

Main point: A diagnosis for PTSD seems extremely high. One must meet all 8 criteria and at least 2 of the additional specifications.

Our goal is not to receive (or avoid) a diagnosis. Our goal is to walk in health. As such, we need to acknowledge that we can still be affected by past events— even if we do not or cannot receive a diagnosis.

Just as most people— even healthy people— can benefit from physical exercise, most can also benefit from some degree of emotional help.

Page: Not in workbook

Talking points: Tell them not to answer aloud, then ask, *Looking at this slide, where would you put yourself on this scale of 0-8?*

If you put yourself anywhere above "0," talk to someone— even if you haven't been diagnosed with PTSD.

Unfortunately, one must meet all criteria to get a diagnosis for PTSD.

Note: you can still be affected even if you don't receive a diagnosis- so it's helpful to assess where you are

Main point: We want to encourage warriors to assess themselves and deal with whatever they discover.

Page: Not in workbook

Talking point: Just because the VA or some other entity will not give a diagnosis, doesn't mean you shouldn't talk to someone or seek help.

2. EMOTIONAL HEALTH

Main point: This slide reminds warriors what has been communicated through this chapter— that emotional health is part of total health.

Page: 51

Talking points: Ask warriors if they would add anything else to this slide. Some responses might include physical exercise, family, financial stability, etc.— suggest some of these if no one responds.

After the discussion, say, "In future chapters we will discuss some of these, such as family and mission."

The goal is not to receive a diagnosis.

The goal is to honestly assess where we are and then walk in health.

Main point: Again, our goal is not to receive (or avoid) a diagnosis. Our goal is to walk in health. As such, we need to acknowledge that we can still be affected by past events— even if we aren't diagnosable.

Page: Not in workbook

Talking points: This is to clarify that we are not licensed medical professionals who are seeking to diagnose, treat, or prescribe. Rather, we are encouraging people to walk in health by encouraging them to ask the tough questions and then equipping them to obtain the resources they need. Remember, the goal is not to get a diagnosis but to get better.

- 66 -

Main point: Emphasize this to the group.

Page: Not in workbook

Talking points: Remind them help can be found in many ways and many places, but we will never find it until we can acknowledge we need help and give ourselves permission to receive it.

Main point: The video / story of John McCarty concludes this lesson.

Page: 59

Talking points: The videos always refer back to the main idea of the chapter, and typically open much dialogue. Leave some time for discussion.

Tell the group to listen as this warrior talks about the difficulty of admitting having problems and needing help.

3. SPIRITUAL HEALTH

YOUR OBJECTIVE: INTRODUCE PARTICIPANTS TO MORAL INJURY (MI)- A CLOSE COUNTER-PART TO PTSD WHICH IS OFTEN MISTAKEN AS MERELY AN EMOTIONAL WOUND. MI HAS MORAL / SPIRITUAL ROOTS.

SPIRITUAL HEALTH

CHAPTER 3

PAGE 63

Main point: Title slide for the lesson.

Page: 63

MAIN IDEA

3. SPIRITUAL HEALTH

WHILE POST-TRAUMATIC STRESS CAN CAUSE EMOTIONAL DISRUPTIONS MANY OF THEM ARE ACTUALLY THE RESULT OF MORAL INJURY. IF SUCH EMOTIONAL TRAUMA IS TREATED AS PTSD THE TREATMENT WILL BE INEFFECTIVE. IT MUST BE CONSIDERED AND APPROACHED DIFFERENTLY.

PAGE 63

Main point: Read the main idea.

Page: 63

Talking points: Ask if the group members have heard of Moral Injury before. If so, ask what they may have heard about it.

(This is also a great time to refer them to the film, *Honoring the Code*. Whereas *Invisible Scars* focuses on PTSD, this second documentary takes a close look at Moral Injury.)

Main point: When we see a sign, we know it isn't there to draw attention to itself but to show us something greater or perhaps warn us.

Page: Slide not in workbook, but page 63 communicates this concept.

Talking points: In the previous lesson we said we could read the signs of PTSD (point 4). This lesson discusses signs of Moral Injury. Though somewhat similar to PTSD, the two are different.

Main point: This is an example of a sign you may encounter in certain parts of the world. In fact, it's can be quite common in some areas.

Page: Slide not in workbook, but the text on page 63 communicates this concept

Talking points: When you come upon this sign at the edge of field, you have a few options— as listed on the sign.

Ask, *Has anyone encountered a sign like this and, if so, how did you respond to it?*

Ask, *Would anyone here simply ignore the sign?*

Whatever you choose, you recognize the sign denotes something dangerous about the field. (How we react may depend on several factors— time we have, is an expert with us, etc.)

You don't make the sign the focus of your attention.

The sign is not about the sign itself

Physical symptoms call our attention to look closer.

Emotional + mental symptoms do the same.

Main point: This reiterates the point we just made.

Page: Slide not in workbook.

Talking points: This is one of the key transitions as you move into the main content of this lesson. And, you might think about it like this:

- A physical symptom— such as blood or intense soreness— causes us to investigate what *that sign* might be showing us (about our physical bodies).

- Emotional symptoms— that is, signs— do the same thing.

Just as we do not ignore the mine field warning, neither should we disregard these signs.

Quick tip: There are four main points in this lesson— you just covered the first. Here they are all together:

1. Signs are not about signs themselves— they point to something we need to know.

2. You're not flawed. The internal unrest you feel is a natural response to the experience you encountered.

3. Moral Injury manifests as feelings of guilt and shame.

4. Experts of diverse backgrounds agree on the "cure."

The key transition in this lesson comes in moving from Point #1 to Point #2. In the same way we see signs in the physical world, Moral Injury also shows us signs.

> ## 2. You're not flawed- the internal unrest you feel is a natural response to the experience you encountered.

Main point: Read the slide.

Page: Slide not in the workbook

Talking points: This is an important distinction to make. The post-war feelings warriors often have don't mark them as "weird" or "flawed."

Internal struggle is a very normal response to the things you've seen and experienced.

Point out the event experienced is what is unnatural— not the feelings you have about it.

After making this observation, give the participants an opportunity to respond to this way of looking at things.

CONSCIENCE

"the sense or consciousness of the moral goodness or blameworthiness of one's own conduct, intentions, or character together with a feeling of obligation to do right or be good."

SOURCE = WEBSTER'S

Main point: We all have a conscience — this is how the dictionary defines it.

Page: The slide is not in the workbook but we define *conscience* on page 64.

Talking points: Notice a few things about the conscience—

- It speaks to good and bad

- It can address what we do (our conduct) and even what we intended to do

- It feels obligated to do good

Main point: Many of us have seen conscience depicted as a cartoon "angel" or "devil," often with one on each shoulder, arguing back and forth.

Page: 65

Talking points: Ask participants if they've ever felt this internal tug-of-war. Most have in some way.

Explain that Moral Injury can result when our conscience is violated— when we are asked or told to do something that violates our own sense of morality.

The next video highlights this.

Main point: This is a video supplied for you to provide the group with an overview of Moral Injury.

Page: 65

Talking points: Dr. Brock, one of the professionals featured in this short clip, is quoted on the next two slides.

"MORAL INJURY RESULTS WHEN SOLDIERS VIOLATE THEIR CORE MORAL BELIEFS, AND IN EVALUATING THEIR BEHAVIOR NEGATIVELY, THEY FEEL THEY NO LONGER LIVE IN A RELIABLE, MEANINGFUL WORLD AND CAN NO LONGER BE REGARDED AS DECENT HUMAN BEINGS. THEY MAY FEEL THIS EVEN IF WHAT THEY DID WAS WARRANTED AND UNAVOIDABLE."

* DR. RITA BROCK

PAGE 65

"THE CONSEQUENCES OF VIOLATING ONE'S CONSCIENCE, EVEN IF THE ACT WAS UNAVOIDABLE OR SEEMED RIGHT AT THE TIME, CAN BE DEVASTATING."

* DR. RITA BROCK

PAGE 65

Main point: Read the quote— a highlight from the previous clip. This is Dr. Brock's summation of Moral Injury.

Page: 65

Talking points: Give the warriors the opportunity to express their thoughts on what she said.

You may simply ask, *Does anyone want to interact with what Dr. Brock is saying?*

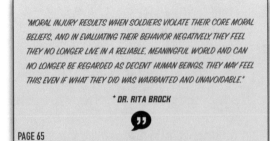

3. Moral Injury manifests as feelings of guilt & shame

Main point: The third point of this lesson.

Page: Not in workbook

Talking points: Guilt and shame are the "signs" that tell us to look inside of ourselves, to take a "deep dive" and explore what's happening inside of us.

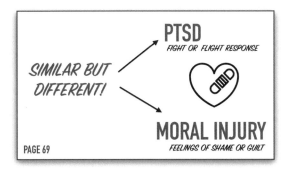

Main point: This slide highlights the difference between PTSD and Moral Injury.

Page: 69

Talking points: PTSD and MI are often lumped together. However, they're different. If you treat MI as if it's PTSD, the treatment will be ineffective.

A key difference is this:

- With PTSD the person is responding to something outside of themselves— an *external* threat resulting in a "fight or flight" response.

- With Moral Injury the threat is *internal,* so warriors feel guilt and/or shame rather than "fight" or "flight."

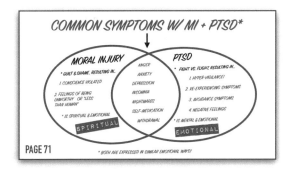

Main point: The symptoms (read: the signs) may look the same. Notice the overlap. But, each of these are different.

Page: 71

Talking point: Be sure and drive home the fact that even though there is some overlap, MI and PTSD are very different.

Point out that many experts— both religious and secular— describe MI as a spiritual concern, a wound that affects our very soul.

Main point: This is a video supplied for you to provide the group with an overview of Moral Injury.

Page: Not in workbook

Talking points: Steven Crutchfield was interviewed for *Invisible Scars*, the film about Post Traumatic Stress. When the producers of the *Invisible Scars* film learned about Moral Injury, they looked back at this footage and thought that it better describes the struggles of Moral Injury than PTSD.

Ask the group, *Do you think what Crutchfield is describing is PTSD or Moral Injury?*

(Note to instructor: He was unable to get a diagnosis for PTSD— probably because he describes Moral Injury.)

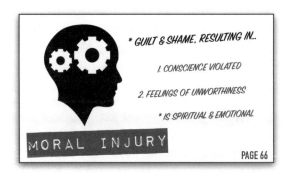

Main point: This is the summary slide for Moral Injury. Notice the differences between this slide and the PTSD slide on page 55 of each participant's manual.

Here is a look at that slide:

Page: 66

GUILT & SHAME		
	BASED ON	**DESCRIBED IN DETAIL**
GUILT	ACTION- "I DID SOMETHING"	SOMETHING YOU DO- IT MAY BE OUT OF CHARACTER FOR YOU, OR COULD HAVE BEEN BASED ON CIRCUMSTANCES
SHAME	IDENTITY- "I AM SOMETHING"	WHO YOU ARE- IT'S DIFFERENT THAN DOING A "BAD THING." THIS DENOTES YOU'RE A BAD PERSON, PERHAPS NOT EVEN VALUED AS A HUMAN

Main point: This slide helps define what guilt and shame are. Whereas guilt is something that most of us feel when we do something that violates our conscience, shame goes much deeper.

Page: Not in workbook

Talking points: Notice that shame coincides with what Dr. Brock said about Moral Injury in the short film clip we watched. Shame cuts to the core of a person's identity, such that they might not feel worthy of even being human.

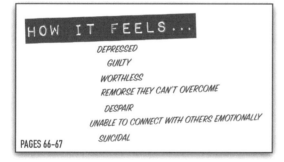

HOW IT FEELS...

DEPRESSED
GUILTY
WORTHLESS
REMORSE THEY CAN'T OVERCOME
DESPAIR
UNABLE TO CONNECT WITH OTHERS EMOTIONALLY
SUICIDAL
PAGES 66-67

Main point: Here's another look at some of the signs of Moral Injury.

Page: Slide not in workbook—concepts are listed in bullet points on pages 66-67

Talking points: Tell the group that if anyone is experiencing these due to an event or action related to their service to not ignore it. Tell them to talk to someone. It is OK to get help.

Let them know you will be glad to talk to them about it, if needed, or direct them to someone else if they prefer.

Main point: Bonus video of J.T. Cooper

Page: Not in workbook

Talking points: This 60-second clip highlights the dilemma many warriors face— when they must perform specific tasks which violate their conscience.

Give the participants a chance to respond to J.T.'s short story here.

> I STARTED HAVING QUESTIONS: "WHAT WAS THE WAR FOR? DID I DO ANY GOOD FOR THIS? COULD WE HAVE DONE SOMETHING DIFFERENTLY? DID WE HAVE TO, YOU KNOW-DID I MAKE A DIFFERENCE IN THIS WAR?"
> MORE IMPORTANTLY, I ASKED MYSELF, "SHOULD I HAVE STAYED OUT OF THE WAR AND WOULD ANYTHING BE DIFFERENT, WOULD EVERYTHING BE BETTER FOR ME IF I HAD?"

PAGE 70

Main point: This quote by a warrior highlights how he began questioning the deeper issues of life.

Notice that therapy, prescriptions… none of the usual PTSD treatments worked.

Page: 70

> NO AMOUNT OF MEDICINE, NO AMOUNT OF THERAPY… NOTHING WORKED. THE DOCTORS DON'T HAVE AN ANSWER TO THAT, NO PRESCRIPTION CAN ANSWER THOSE QUESTIONS. THE ONLY THING I CAN DO IS REALLY WORK WITH OTHER VETERANS, OR CHAPLAINS TO TRY AND GET THOSE ANSWERS.
>
> **✝ KYLE RADKE, AIR FORCE CAPTAIN**
>
>

PAGES 70

Talking points: Captain Radke struggled with his involvement in the war— did it help, should we have been there, etc.

Ask the warriors, *Have you ever known someone that has experienced this— perhaps yourself?*

If any of them have, ask, *Would you mind sharing that story?*

Note that Captain Radke was diagnosed with and treated for PTSD, but later realized he actually had Moral Injury— this is why the treatment for PTSD was ineffective.

4. Experts of multiple diverse backgrounds agree on the "cure."

Main point: The fourth and final point of the lesson

Page: Not in workbook

FORGIVENESS = FREEDOM

PAGE 74

Main point: Guilt and shame cannot exist in the light of forgiveness.

Page: 74

Talking points: Point out that whereas guilt and shame grow— and increase in intensity— when they are not addressed, when exposed to acceptance and forgiveness by others and by yourself they fade away.

THE HINDRANCE =

GUILT
I DID SOMETHING SO HORRIBLE IT CAN'T BE FORGIVEN

SHAME
I AM HORRIBLE- WHAT WOULD PEOPLE THINK OF ME IF THEY KNEW?

Main point: Guilt and shame love to hide in the dark— to remain your secret to deal with. Sometimes, this is a false guilt or shame that we don't need to feel.

Page: Not in workbook

Talking points: Point out the difference between guilt (feelings about something I did) and shame (feelings about self, because of something I did). Be sure and point out that sometimes we take on a guilt or shame that is not ours to carry, as it is for something we didn't do. (Survivor's guilt is one example.)

FORGIVENESS
A PASTOR, A PRIEST OR A RABBI
A FORMER COACH
AN OFFICER THEY SERVED UNDER
A BATTLE-BUDDY
SOMEONE ELSE PERCEIVED AS AN AUTHORITY

Main point: Experts agree the person imparting forgiveness doesn't have to be a religious leader. They simply must be someone the person believes has the moral authority to impart forgiveness.

Page: Slide not in workbook, but these relationships are listed on page 73.

Talking points: It seems like a simple answer, but the data is consistent. Practitioners of healing who have studied MI— from both secular and sacred sources— agree that overcoming MI requires receiving forgiveness from someone the warrior believes has the moral authority to forgive.

State, *If you need forgiveness picture in your mind who you believe can give this to you. Determine to go to them ASAP.*

It is when this forgiveness is given and received that the healing process often begins.

For example, Captain Radke discovered he had Moral Injury by reading the Bible and seeking the counsel of his chaplain and other spiritual leaders. Then, he understood his need for forgiveness.

Main point: The video for this lesson comes from Maj. Gen. Jim Mukoyama.

Page: His story is found on page 76.

Talking points: Mukoyama believes that Moral Injury, first and foremost, must be treated as a matter of the soul, a spiritual issue. Based on this belief he has established Military Outreach USA, an organization that helps those who suffer from Moral Injury.

Main point: Remind warriors that the documentaries are available for them if they wish to renew these concepts farther.

Page: Not in workbook

4. DEFINING THE MISSION

YOUR OBJECTIVE: ENCOURAGE WARRIORS TO PLAN THEIR LIFE WITH THE SAME INTENSITY AND DETAIL THEY USED TO PLAN MILITARY MISSIONS.

Main point: Title slide for the lesson.

Page: 81

Quick tip: With this lesson we shift to Unit 2 of the manual, Opportunity. Before moving through the content of this chapter, take a few minutes to review the previous Unit, to show warriors how this lesson fits with the bigger picture.

Main point: This is the recap of Unit 1 — chapters 1 (Mental Health), 2 (Emotional Health), and 3 (Spiritual Health).

Page: Slide not in workbook.

Talking point: This is what we just covered for the previous three lessons.

Main point: This is the overview of this Unit. This is what we will cover in this lesson and the following two lessons.

Page: Slide not in workbook.

Talking point: As we move into Unit 2, Opportunity, we're going to discuss moving forward. It doesn't mean we "forget" about the previous Unit. But, now that we have the tools to deal with the invisible scars of the past, we begin stepping forward.

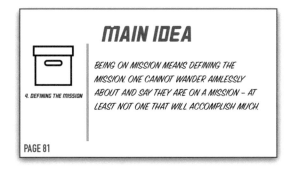

Main point: Read the main idea.

Page: 81

Talking points: Ask the group to talk about military missions in which they participated— and share some of the ingredients necessary for success.

Responses may include planning, equipment, leadership, clear objectives, etc.

Ask, *Did every mission work exactly as planned?*

Few of them do. The same is true of life missions. Point out that while we certainly want every mission to be perfect, that is not necessary for success. Even when the mission gets "a little messy," it can still work. The same is true of life missions.

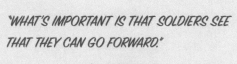

Main point: Read the quote.

Page: 79

Talking points: This is an important point: the warrior needs to be able to move forward. Yet, when many warriors arrive home they can't see a future and, therefore, have difficulty seeing any present opportunities.

Ask, *Do you agree that many warriors return home and have no idea what to do now— what's next in life?*

Ask if anyone knows of an example of this happening in a warrior's life.

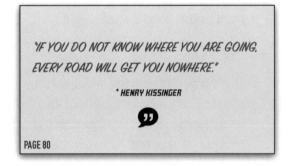

Main point: Dr. Kissinger is saying, "If you don't have a plan, you'll end up nowhere." So, if you want to end up "somewhere," it's important to move forward— but do so with a plan, a purpose, a mission.

Page: 80

Talking points: The purpose of this chapter is to encourage warriors to step forward with intentionality— with a plan, even if it's not a perfect one.

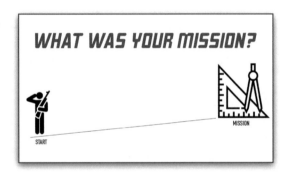

Main point: Let's compare this concept of living with an intentional plan to your time in the service.

Page: Slide not in workbook, but this concept is on page 82 of the book.

Talking points: Ask warriors, *What was your mission in the military?*

Most will readily answer, giving you differing ideas on what they did— with much detail and precision.

After the discussion calms and everyone who wants to talk has a chance to do so, ask, *How many of you have a mission like that for your present life?*

Main point: This is the cover image for a short film clip about the "transcendent cause." Listen to how General Boykin describes this.

Page: Slide not in workbook, but there is a quote from Boykin on page 84— and the transcendent cause graphic is on page 86.

Talking points: This video flows into the next slide.

Main point: This is the follow-up to the video.

Page: 86

Talking points: Discuss the transcendent cause concept as it relates to the military— of being a part of something larger than one's self, of having a purpose.

Ask, *Did you have a sense of a transcendent cause when you were serving? Was this concept part of your training?*

Then, after discussing, ask, *Is there a transcendent cause for life after the military?*

Ask, *Can you think of some examples?*

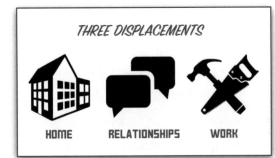

Main point: Many return from military service and feel displaced.

Page: Slide not in workbook.

Talking points: There may be other displacements, but some which seem the most apparent are these—

- Home = the family learns to function (by necessity) without the warrior.

- Relationships = people have integrated into their own "web" while the service member has been away.

- Work = they may have to learn a new skill set, as things have changed. Or, they may have been leading at an extremely high level — overseeing massive logistics— only to return to something that seems far less important.

Ask, *Who has felt displaced since returning from service?*

If hands are raised, remind them this is normal and ask if anyone would like to share about their experience.

Main point. Finding a purpose is one essential ingredient in recovering and moving forward— to feeling like you have a place (not feeling displaced).

Page: Slide not in workbook.

Main point: In the same way warriors defined clear objectives and created strategies to achieve them, they can do the same with any area of life.

Page: 82

Talking points: It's important for you — that your energy is focused in the right direction. Doing this is also important for others— for the people who benefit from your efforts.

If you simply do a lot of things in life, you will certainly accomplish something. However, if you focus your activity on an objective (target), you will accomplish what is best for you and those around you.

Main point: A mission clarifies what the target— or objective— is.

Page: Slide not in workbook.

Talking points: Ask, *Who has thought of their life as a mission?*

Warriors need to think about using their training and ability to follow through to achieve life objectives.

If we wander through life we will end up somewhere, but will it be the place we want to be? Point out that the warrior needs a life mission.

Ask, *Are you aiming at a target— a goal— or just wandering aimlessly?*

NO MISSION =
POST-MILITARY SHOCK

Main point: Many warriors feel "in shock" when they take off the uniform because they no longer have that mission. Whereas they used to wake up each day with clear goals and a schedule that was highly regimented, this is often no longer the case post-military.

Page: Slide not in workbook.

NO MISSION =
POST-MILITARY SHOCK
BUT...
Did you have one pre-military, or did finally having a mission awaken the need for one in you?

Main point: The question on the bottom half of the slide is key— most young people typically do not have a mission, due to their age and life situation.

However, most warriors enlist when they are extremely young, and the military awakens that need for a mission— a purpose. Having this mission becomes a critical part of their life.

Page: Slide not in workbook.

Talking points: Emphasize that this new mindset (to have a mission) is a great gift the military gave them— and it can work in other areas of life, as well.

In fact, we're designed to live with purpose and intentionality. And, their training can help find it.

Quick tip: Remember the two-fold objective we outlined during the introductory week (see page 19):

- Find healing

- Find a mission

Both are important aspects of life— and will continue to be so well into the future.

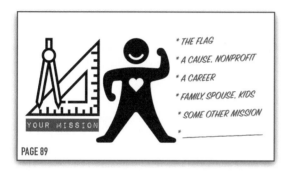

Main point: The mission can be anything larger than the person— something that is a "transcendent cause" for now. This slide contains a few examples.

Page: 89

Talking points: Notice a few points about the next mission—

- It can be varied— just about anything can qualify

- The mission generally involves other people— and includes serving them in some way

- There may be multiple missions for each warrior

- There may be multiple warriors for each mission— just as when you served

Main point: This is the lead image from the video of J.T. Cooper's story.

Page: J.T.'s story begins on page 89.

Talking point: Notice how J.T. shifted his focus from one thing to the next in his story, using his training to continue moving forward.

5. OVERCOMING OBSTACLES

YOUR OBJECTIVE: ENCOURAGE WARRIORS THAT LIFE MISSIONS— JUST LIKE MILITARY MISSIONS— NEVER HAPPEN EXACTLY AS PLANNED. HOWEVER, WE CAN ADJUST AND STILL MOVE FORWARD TO OUR GOAL.

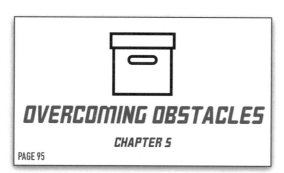

Main point: Title slide for chapter 5

Page: 95

Quick tip: Military personnel are trained not to look back and consider how much ground they have covered, but to continue looking forward only.

In this lesson we are going to encourage them to do something that seems counter to that training when we suggest that they not only evaluate "how much father" it is until they reach their goal, but that they also look back to celebrate— and remember- how much progress they've made.

We refer to this as the *gap* ("how much farther?") and the *gain* ("look how far we've already come!").

> "THERE'S LIKELY A PLACE IN PARADISE FOR PEOPLE WHO TRIED HARD, BUT WHAT REALLY MATTERS IS SUCCEEDING. IF THAT REQUIRES YOU TO CHANGE, THAT'S YOUR MISSION."
>
> + GENERAL STANLEY MCCHRYSTAL, U.S. ARMY RETIRED

PAGE 94

Main point: Read the quote from the workbook.

Page: 95

Talking point: Ask, *What do you think about the McChrystal's statement?*

Continuing— and completing— the mission is essential training for warriors— even if it means adapting to a changing situation. We want to remind them of this, and that it can be lived in a healthy way for all aspects of life.

PAGE 95

Main point: Show the slide and ask if anyone has seen this sign before— and what it means.

Page: 95

Talking point: Ask, *What do you typically think when you come to an unexpected detour sign— especially if you're in an unfamiliar area?*

Some of the answers should include:

- I might be late

- I hope I don't get lost

- I hope there are good directions

Ask, *What would happen if every time you came to a detour you stopped your trip?*

Point out that no one likes to encounter a detour.

Quick tip: This focus of this lesson is encouraging warriors to continue moving forward on their mission— even if that means they must adapt. In the same way we sometimes make adjustments when driving, we must also made adjustments in life. The detour sign on a road promises that we'll still arrive at our intended destination— if we stay on the road. The same is true in life. We only fail when we stop making forward progress.

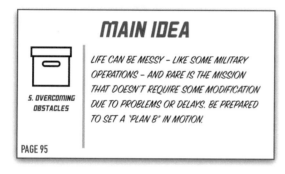

MAIN IDEA

5. OVERCOMING OBSTACLES

LIFE CAN BE MESSY - LIKE SOME MILITARY OPERATIONS - AND RARE IS THE MISSION THAT DOESN'T REQUIRE SOME MODIFICATION DUE TO PROBLEMS OR DELAYS. BE PREPARED TO SET A "PLAN B" IN MOTION.

PAGE 95

Main point: Read the main idea.

Page: 95

Talking point: Ask the warriors, *Did any of you ever have a mission that went sideways? Did you ever have to make adjustments?*

If— and when— they answer affirmatively, give them the opportunity to share a time when that happened.

(If no one speaks up, you can share a personal story or encourage them to share one that they've heard from another warrior.)

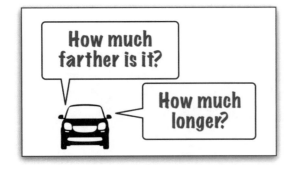

Main point: If you have kids or have been a kid you can probably relate to this.

Page: Slide not in workbook.

Talking point: In the same way kids do this in the car, adults often do this in life. We, too, can grow discouraged when we don't see the destination as soon as we thought we would.

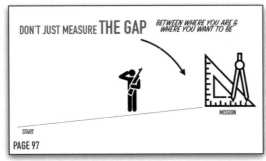
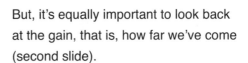

Main point: It's important to live in reality, and realize how much farther we need to progress before we arrive at our destination. This is the gap between where we are and where we want to be (first slide).

But, it's equally important to look back at the gain, that is, how far we've come (second slide).

(These two slides work together.)

Page: 97-98

Talking point: Ask if they were trained not to "look back" in service. If they answer affirmatively, ask *why.*

(They may have been taught the mission is always ahead.)

Ask, *Why is it good to look back in life?*

Be sure and clarify we "look back" to celebrate how far we've come— not to dwell on past hurts, pains, and mistakes, even though these may be part of and help our progress.

DON'T GET STUCK IN THE "MESSY MIDDLE"

★ DETERMINE TO GET ON MISSION
★ HAVE A PLAN THAT WILL GUIDE YOU
★ BELIEVE IN YOURSELF AND WHERE YOU'RE HEADED
★ PERIODICALLY CHECK YOUR MAP
★ CELEBRATE HOW FAR YOU'VE COME
★ COMMIT TO BEING EVEN FARTHER DOWN THE ROAD TOMORROW
★ BE WILLING TO MAKE ADJUSTMENTS - OBSTACLES ARE A GIVEN

Main point: When between the starting point and finish line, it's easy to get stuck in the "messy middle"— that place where you're neither at your starting point or your goal (you've stopped moving, having made too much progress to start over, yet you're still a significant distance from your goal).

Ask, *Have any of you ever felt like that — in any area of life?*

Page: Slide not in workbook, but the concept is discussed on pages 98-99.

Talking point: The "messy middle" is similar to what marathon runners sometimes refer to as "hitting the wall" — the point where you feel like quitting but may just need to regroup and push forward.

Remind them that it's natural to feel some tension when you're in "the land in between."

The points on this slide outline some practical tips for living in that "messy middle."

Notice the final point— obstacles are a certainty.

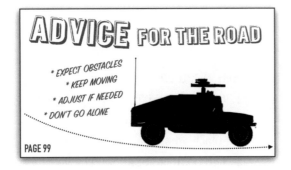

Main point: Here's some advice as you move from where you are to where you're destined to be.

Page: 99

Talking point: Notice that the four points reiterate the main idea of the lesson— about expecting obstacles.

- Remind warriors that they will face various obstacles. Don't be surprised when they do.

- Furthermore, these points remind us what we learned about detours — even though we face them we can still get to our destination— if we continue moving.

- Sometimes, we just need to adjust the path we take.

- And, the final point is something we'll discuss in chapter 6— in the same way you don't do military missions alone you shouldn't do life missions alone, either.

Quick tip: The next few slides will discuss the inevitable obstacles we face— that is, the things which necessitate course corrections and detours. Review pages 105-109 during your preparation time to teach the following:

- The first slide lists all of the obstacles we will discuss (left side = obstacles that are common to all, including warriors; right side = additional obstacles related to PTSD & MI)

- The second slide will focus on the left (those common to all)

- The third slide will focus on the right (those specifically related to PTSD & MI)

OBSTACLES

A. COMMON TO ALL	B. RELATED TO THE EFFECTS OF POST-TRAUMATIC STRESS & MORAL INJURY
1. NOT HAVING A PLAN	
2. TRYING TO TAKE TOO MUCH GROUND AT ONCE	1. REINTEGRATION INTO CIVILIAN LIFE
3. STOPPING SHORT OF THE OBJECTIVE	2. ISOLATION & WITHDRAWAL FROM HELP
4. PHYSICAL LIMITATIONS	3. ADDICTIONS
5. LETTING THE PAST DETERMINE THE PRESENT	4. SUICIDAL THOUGHTS

PAGE 101

Main point: This is a summary slide of all of the obstacles listed

Page: 101

Talking point: Let's break these down and look at both categories.

OBSTACLES

A. COMMON TO ALL

1. NOT HAVING A PLAN
2. TRYING TO TAKE TOO MUCH GROUND AT ONCE
3. STOPPING SHORT OF THE OBJECTIVE
4. PHYSICAL LIMITATIONS
5. LETTING THE PAST DETERMINE THE PRESENT

PAGE 104

Main point: Refer to the list of obstacles which are common to all people.

Page: 104

Talking point: Notice the following about each of the obstacles listed—

1. You can name a destination, but if you don't have a plan it will be more difficult and take much longer to achieve.

2. It's better to do a little bit each day than try to achieve everything at once— first, do what you can accomplish. Remember Admiral McRaven's advice to make your bed on page 102 of the Basic Manual.

3. Aim to cross the goal line— do not stop short.

4. Sometimes there are physical limitations— especially among warriors. Physical injuries that occur during service can limit or hinders one's abilities.

5. We need to move beyond the past. We are no longer hindered or restrained by it— don't let the past become an anchor that holds you back.

Give warriors the opportunity to share their thoughts about any of these obstacles.

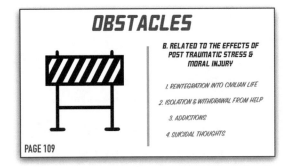

Main point: Refer to the list of obstacles which are specific to PTSD & MI.

Page: 109

Talking point: Ask the warriors, *What do you think causes these obstacles?*

1. *Why is it difficult to reintegrate?*

2. *Why do warriors withdraw from help?*

3. *Why do warriors turn to addictions?*

4. *Why do 22 warriors per day choose suicide?*

Ask, *What should people do who are facing these obstacles?*

Main point: Refer back to the slide we showed at the beginning of the lesson.

Page: 95

Talking point: Ask the warriors, *What are some of your takeaways from this lesson?*

Main point: Sgt. Horace Lee is a Marine who served in the Pacific during World War II.

Page: His story is found on page 110.

Talking point: Tell the group to listen specifically for how Sgt. Lee deals with past thoughts that pop up to haunt him. We'll talk about this in more detail in chapter 7, "Facing the Past."

6. PARTNERING WITH OTHERS

YOUR OBJECTIVE: ONE OF THE MOST MEMORABLE POINTS OF MILITARY SERVICE WAS THE CAMARADERIE SHARED WITH OTHER WARRIORS. REMIND WARRIORS THAT THIS IS AN ASPECT OF PAST EXPERIENCE THAT SHOULD BE NURTURED POST-MILITARY, AS WELL.

PARTNERING WITH OTHERS
CHAPTER 6
PAGE 115

Main point: Title slide for chapter 6

Page: 115

Quick tip: Warriors often point to past military experience and recall the days of walking closely with others for whom they had great admiration and with whom they shared deep mutual trust. Though it takes time to build solid relationships, these are aspects of life that warriors need to develop as they move forward into their next mission.

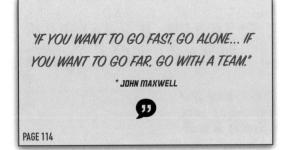

Main point: Read the quote.

Page: 114

Talking points: Many people will relate to this slide. It's often easier to simply "do it yourself."

Whereas doing it yourself ensures it will be done as you want it to be done, doing it yourself also has drawbacks.

You become the "lid." When you fail to involve others, you limit your capacity by excluding other options that would allow you to outgrow or outpace what you're able achieve on your own.

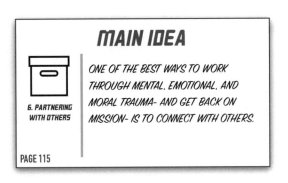

Main point: Read the main point of the lesson.

Page: 115

Talking points: Notice that people are involved in multiple aspects of our lives.

- Relationships are one of the best means to move forward from past hurts and find healing.

- Relationship are also one of the best means to move forward and walk in health.

Ask, *What would life be like if you had to live alone?*

Keep in mind this may be the situation for some in your group.

Quick tip: When they get out of service, warriors are often hesitant to trust other people. This may seem odd, considering in service they literally had to entrust their lives to others, in many cases.

"Relational trust" is a high level decision for them, so the question is often *Can they find it outside of the military?*

On some level, you might need to discuss with them that relationships are essential— and we may trust certain people more, depending on how close they are to us. It's OK to grant different levels of trust to others.

PAGE 115

Main point: We're designed to connect.

Page: 115

Talking points: Ask the group which ones of these is true: *Do birds of a feather flock together or do opposites attract?*

You may receive various responses. Some people may even seem confused, because they've never heard these two "contradictory" observations placed side-by-side before.

Explain that both of these statements are true. We do tend to gather with people who are like us. But in some instances we also contact with those who are unlike us. Anyone married knows this to be true.

The bigger issue, though, is that— whatever the case— we're drawn to connect with other people.

Main point: Practically every warrior, no matter their branch of service, can relate to "having someone's six."

Page: 114

Talking points: Ask, *What does this mean to you?*

After they answer, follow-up with, *Who has your six?*

Some participants may mention specific people; others may look to the past, suggesting that no one currently has their six. It's important to remember that in order for someone to have your six, you must also be willing to have theirs. Relationships work both ways.

Main point: A shield wall works because those who form it maintain their position. Each person protects the space directly in front of them, and the warriors to their right and left. If one falls or leaves the group, those on either side become vulnerable.

Page: 118

Talking points: In a shield wall, everyone is protected, or everyone is vulnerable. There is no "in between."

Ask the warriors if they ever experienced a time in service when they felt that their safety or success was dependent on who was to their side.

If so, ask them if they've felt this way since leaving the military.

Main point: We viewed this short clip about having a transcendent cause in chapter 4.

Page: Slide not in workbook, but this information is on pages 119-120.

Talking points: In light of this discussion, let's consider again what General Boykin said about having a transcendent cause.

Remind warriors that even in battle, the war wasn't just about the war. It was about the people closest to them. It is common for warriors to communicate that the *essence* of the military is the person beside you.

Main point: Who are you with?

Page: Slide not in workbook. See pages 121-122 for information.

Talking points: Ask the warriors what might happen if—

- *If warriors continued to be a "shield wall" for their battle buddies in fighting PTSD and Moral Injury?*

- *If warriors continued being on mission together?*

Review Jim Collins' concept about "who before what" on pages 121-122 (continued on next page).

Communicate the following:

- Biggest difference between good companies and great companies— the leader.

- Biggest factor in making the company great— the leader invested in people even before pursuing projects.

Main point: Draw the warriors attention to this long-used military transport— sometimes referred to as a "deuce-and-a-half" (2.5-ton truck).

Page: 121

Talking points: Ask them what the most important aspect of that vehicle is — its destination, its design, or the people onboard?

Jim Collins' conclusion was that the right group of people always make the "bus" work and they always make sure it arrives at its best possible destination. That is why having the right people on the bus— or, in this case, the transport— is a necessity.

Illustrate this by asking how successful your mission to take an enemy's position would be if everyone on your transport was a medic.

Then, *How successful would it be without a medic?*

3 IMPORTANT TEAMS

1. FELLOW VETERANS / "BATTLE BUDDIES"

2. SERVICE PROVIDERS - ORGANIZATIONS THAT PROVIDE ASSISTANCE FOR VETERANS

3. FAMILY AND FRIENDS - THOSE WHO MOST WANT TO SEE HEALING & RESTORATION TAKE PLACE.

PAGE 123

Main point: Notice that the bus is a small vehicle. We can't maintain close proximity with everyone we know as they won't all fit on the bus. It is important to focus on the right people — those who must be on that "bus."

Page: 123

Talking points: Notice the three groups that must be present as you move forward.

Ask, *Why is it important for each group on the slide to be onboard?*

Follow-up: *What can you do to maintain your connection with them?*

Stress that you cannot get everyone on the bus, so make sure you have the right people.

Who is on your bus?
Who needs to be?

Main point: The information about relationships isn't new. Most warriors have experienced this degree of trust before. However, most of them are not walking in it at this point, and are therefore limited in the amount of healing they have experienced and the magnitude of the mission they can carry.

Page: Slide not in workbook

(Talking points on next page.)

Talking points: Use this as an opportunity to allow the warriors to share what they have learned.

Ask if any are willing to share some specific personal examples of what they have learned or how this concept may have helped them personally.

Main point: Dr. Sarah Gilliam is a psychologist who deals with mental and emotional trauma soldiers develop while in combat. She is also the wife of a combat soldier with several deployments. Here is her story about how the family is also affected by a spouse's unresolved PTSD and Moral Injury.

Page: Her story is found on page 127.

> "LAST NIGHT I WATCHED THE FILM INVISIBLE SCARS WITH MY WIFE. WHEN IT ENDED SHE TURNED TO ME AND SAID, 'NOW, I GET IT.'"
>
> + VIETNAM VET

PAGE 126

Main point: One of the three groups who must be on the bus is "family." Yet it's often difficult to share with family members.

Page: Slide not in workbook— this quote is found on page 126, however.

Talking points: If they can't or don't know how to help family members understand what they're dealing with, suggest to warriors that show them the *Invisible Scars* and *Honoring the Code* documentaries.

Main point: This slide is placed for your convenience to remind them of the two films, as well as the difference between them.

Page: 126

Main point: As you conclude the lesson, remind the participates to connect with one another— and through the Facebook group.

Page: Slide not in workbook.

7. FACING THE PAST

YOUR OBJECTIVE: HELP WARRIORS IDENTIFY ANYTHING ANCHORING THEM TO THE PAST AND PREVENTING THEM FROM MOVING FORWARD IN FREEDOM.

Main point: Title slide for chapter 7

Page: 135

Quick tip: With chapter 7 we move into a new unit, Peace.

- Healing (Unit 1 = H) comprised chapters 1-3.

- Opportunity (Unit 2= O) comprised chapters 4-6.

- Peace (Unit 3= P) comprises chapters 7-9.

Quickly review the previous units using the following slides. Don't spend too much time on these, as you have a lot of information to cover in this chapter.

H -> HEALING

O -> OPPORTUNITY

P -> PEACE

E -> EMPOWERMENT

Main point: This slide provides the group with an overview of the book—all four units.

Page: Slide not in workbook. You may want to refer to the Table of Contents, however, on pages 5-6.

Talking points: We are now in the unit that focuses on peace. But first, let's quickly review the ground we've covered.

HEALING

* MENTAL
* EMOTIONAL
* SPIRITUAL

Main point: Unit 1 covered three chapters on healing— mentally, emotionally, and physically.

Page: Slide not in workbook.

Talking points: Ask the group if anyone would like to share one of their biggest takeaways from that section— or even share something that has changed in light of what they learned.

OPPORTUNITY

* DEFINE THE MISSION
* OVERCOME OBSTACLES
* PARTNER WITH OTHERS

Main point: Unit 2 covered three chapters on opportunity—

- We learned that we can define life missions in the same way we outlined military missions.

- We acknowledged that nothing ever goes exactly as planned.

- We reminded ourselves that the best part of any plan is the people who are involved.

Page: Slide not in workbook.

Talking points: Ask the group if anyone would like to share a highlight from that section of the book.

PEACE

* FACING THE PAST
* OWNING THE PRESENT
* EMBRACING THE FUTURE

Main point: This is the overview for this entire unit. We'll discuss the first aspect, facing the past, in this lesson.

Page: Slide not in workbook.

Talking points: Ask the group, *Do you think people get nervous when we bring up the past? And, if so, why?*

A follow-up is, *Can we learn good things from the past while also addressing some of the hurts— can we find benefit in both— the good and the pain?*

> "THE TRUTH IS, UNLESS YOU LET GO, UNLESS YOU FORGIVE YOURSELF, UNLESS YOU FORGIVE THE SITUATION, UNLESS YOU REALIZE THAT THE SITUATION IS OVER, YOU CANNOT MOVE FORWARD."
>
> † STEVE MARABOLI
>
>
>
> PAGE 134

Main point: Read the quote and tell the warriors that sometimes the biggest obstacle to moving beyond the past is ourselves— this goes back to what we learned about PTSD and Moral Injury.

Page: 134

Talking points: The only part of the past we can really control— or do anything about— is how we choose to deal with it ourselves. We can:

- Seek healing from the things we need healing from

- Learn the lessons— good and bad — that we can take with us

Quick tip: (Remind warriors that when we mention "the past," we often automatically think in negative terms. Whereas we need to deal with the tough parts of the past, we need to remember there are some great moments there, too.)

Dealing with the past doesn't mean we deny— or forget— the hard parts of it. Rather, it means we no longer allow it to define us and dictate what we can do.

MAIN IDEA

7. FACING THE PAST

HOW ONE DEALS WITH THE PAST CAN HAVE A DRAMATIC IMPACT ON HOW THEY LIVE IN THE PRESENT. IF A PAST EVENT HAS BECOME AN ANCHOR THAT KEEPS YOU FROM MOVING FORWARD, IT MUST BE ADDRESSED.

PAGE 135

Main point: Read the main idea for this lesson.

Page: 135

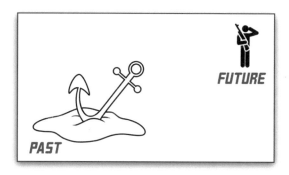

Main point: This slide represents the goal— to step into the future.

Page: Slide not in workbook

Talking points: Tell participants this, "Don't answer this question unless you feel comfortable doing so— just think about it: *What hinders you from moving forward to the future?"*

After giving them some time to think (or even talk about it), say, "For many warriors, the answer is their past."

Main point: This slide is often the reality— something keeps us anchored, tethered to previous chapters of our life.

Page: Slide not in workbook

Talking points: Ask the warriors, *What are some of the events, memories, etc., that might be keeping warriors anchored to the past?*

We'll consider what to do about these as we move forward in this chapter.

Main point: Ask, *When you look at the image on this slide what comes to mind?*

- For some it means victory.

- For some it is a symbol of peace.

Perhaps, both came to mind. Victory and peace *should* be inseparable.

Page: 135

Talking points: The natural end to war should be a victory that achieves a sustainable peace. But, after the fighting ends and peace is achieved by the nations involved, many warriors return home *without* personal peace— they are still fighting a war inside.

The conflict stays with many of them, because it is embedded in their memory where they re-live it.

Consider the following statement.

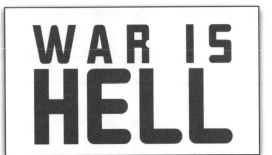

Main point: The thing that often keeps warriors from moving forward is trauma related to their service experience.

This slide is part of a quote from General Sherman. He reflected on the savagery of war, and the toll it takes on people— particularly warriors.

Page: Slide not in workbook— content on page 139.

Talking points: Ask, *Do you agree with General Sherman? If so, why?*

One of the concepts we've discussed in this manual is that many of the reactions warriors have after deployment are natural responses to what they have experienced. Deployment can take a toll on a person.

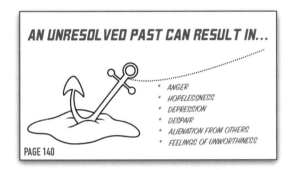

Main point: An unresolved past can eat at your soul and become unbearable. No matter how much time passes it remains a fresh wound that the warrior may have to deal with.

Page: 140

Talking points: Ask the warriors if they've personally encountered or perhaps know a warrior who has encountered any of these feelings. Ask if they can identify why these may crop up even years after serving.

Main point: This slide reminds warriors that war is heroic… and it's hard. It takes a toll on the warrior. Many people do not see this, but it's normal to have things reminding us of or tethering us the past. We need to deal with them.

Page: 141

Talking points: Ask, *How do you think about the statement on the slide?*

Do you agree that someone who hasn't served thinks of war differently?

Point out that those who haven't served often ask, "Did you kill anyone?" And, "How many?"

They don't mean anything by it, but such questions remind us— or tether us— to those past events.

Ask, *Has anyone every been asked this? How does it make you feel?*

Main point: Here are a few practical tips for letting go of the past.

Page: 142

Talking points: Here are three practical tips:

1. The past doesn't have to determine how a warrior lives in the present.

2. The past shouldn't be forgotten. Burying pain doesn't help. It simply guarantees that the pain may come back again in the future. There are also great moments of the past that need to be remembered.

3. If your mind gets stuck on a destructive memory you need a substitute to put in its place and move you towards something positive. Think of what Horace Lee said about "turning the page" (page 110, Chapter 5, Overcoming Obstacles).

Main point: Illustrate Lee's point by showing this slide and asking the group what they see.

Page: Slide not in workbook

Talking points: Then, tell them, *I want you to close your eyes— and not think about a pink elephant.*

Tell them again, *Do not think about a pink elephant.*

After a few seconds ask them what they were thinking about. Most will have thought about a pink elephant.

The more we try to "stuff" something, the more we actually think about it.

(Continued on next page.)

When our past is the "elephant in the room," it works the same way as this exercise. One of the most effective ways to stop thinking about something is think about something else that's positive.

"WHATEVER THINGS ARE TRUE, WHATEVER THINGS ARE NOBLE, WHATEVER THINGS ARE JUST, WHATEVER THINGS ARE PURE, WHATEVER THINGS ARE LOVELY, WHATEVER THINGS ARE OF GOOD REPORT, IF THERE IS ANY VIRTUE AND IF THERE IS ANYTHING PRAISEWORTHY- MEDITATE ON THESE THINGS."

- PHILIPPIANS 4:8

PAGE 140

Main point: This quote is by the Apostle Paul, a follower of Jesus who experienced many devastating life events such as imprisonment, beatings, multiple attacks by robbers, shipwrecks, being left for dead, and many other things. He acknowledged these in many of his writings.

Page: 140

Talking points: In this quote Paul is not saying to pretend bad events didn't happen or aren't part of who you are. Rather, he is saying not to dwell on them nor to keep thinking about them— like Horace Lee said.

Think about the positive.

Ask the warriors for a few ways they can shift their thinking— how they can "turn the page"— when they "get stuck." It might involve a specific action they do, thoughts they remind themselves of… the goal is let them share possible "turn the page" solutions with each other.

Main point: This is a reminder of something we continue highlighting—all of our past isn't bad.

Page: 144

Talking points: Amidst the pain there are some incredible gifts we need to remember.

- There are great memories

- There are great people

This will lead us into the video by Washington Booker III.

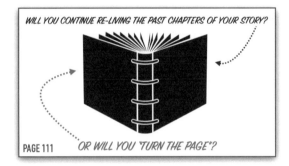

Main point: Ask the warriors if they are ready to "turn the page"?

Page: 111

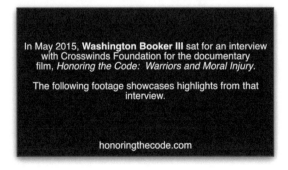

Main point: This is a video clip of Washington Booker. Notice how he recalls both hurtful memories and vividly good ones in the same story—even in his time of combat.

Page: His story is found on page 110.

8. OWNING THE PRESENT

YOUR OBJECTIVE: ENCOURAGE WARRIORS TO STRIVE TO LIVE FULLY PRESENT, AND TO BE ACTIVELY ENGAGED IN THE MOMENT.

Main point: Title slide for chapter 8

Page: 149

Quick tip: We don't want people to negate the past and act as if it never happened. Nor do we want them to be so future-oriented that they forget about the present.

Past, present, and future all have their place in our lives. We must be careful that one does not become so dominant that it closes the door on the others.

"WHEN OBSTACLES ARISE, YOU CHANGE YOUR DIRECTION TO REACH YOUR GOAL; YOU DO NOT CHANGE YOUR DECISION TO GET THERE."

* ZIG ZIGLAR, MOTIVATIONAL SPEAKER & WWII VETERAN

Main point: Read the quote.

Page: 196 (the back of the book, just before the Field Notes)

Talking points: Remind the warriors that we considered obstacles for an entire chapter (5). We learned that we should expect them. When we do, we don't change our mind about our future goals, we just adjust what we do in the present moment so we might still accomplish them.

MAIN IDEA

8. OWNING THE PRESENT

TAKING OWNERSHIP OF THE PRESENT OFTEN MEANS ONE MUST LET GO OF THE PAST. TO LET GO OF THE PAST YOU MUST DETERMINE TO LIVE IN THE PRESENT. MOVING FORWARD IS INTENTIONAL. IT REQUIRES MAKING A CONSCIOUS DECISION.

PAGE 149

Main point: Read the main point for this chapter.

Page: 149

Talking points: Notice that staying engaged in the present is an ongoing decision. We must decide every day— often times, many times in a day— to stay engaged.

Our goal is not just to stumble forward aimlessly, but to move with planned precision.

Main point: It's difficult to live "fully present" when we're tethered to something in the past.

Page: Not in workbook. You will find similar slides in the previous chapter, however, on pages 140 and 142.

Talking points: Remember, as we saw on page 97 of the manual, looking back may seem counter-intuitive to your service training which may have taught you *not* to look back and potentially lose time or even get left behind. That may certainly be true on a combat mission, but *now* we are talking about life situations, particularly those impacted by mental, emotional, and moral trauma.

Main point: Our past has brought us to where we are.

Page: Not in workbook, but similar slides on pages 140 and 142.

Talking point: Having broken the chain of the past, we need to live and engage the present, because that is what will create the best possible future for us.

Quick tip: We don't want to full review every lesson, but we do want to tie the main ideas together when it's expedient to do so.

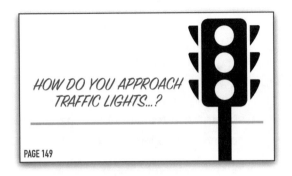

Main point: Show the slide and ask the group, *What do you do when you come to a traffic light?*

The answer should be that it depends on the color of the light.

Page: 149

Talking points: Make sure the following points are discussed:

- Some approach yellow lights more cautiously; others approach more aggressively.

- We all know to stop at red and go at green, however.

Main point: Most people have found themselves stuck at a red light that won't seem to change.

Page: 151

Talking point: Ask, *What do you do if you're stopped at a red light and feel it has been red too long? Would you go on through it or keep waiting? What if no one else is around?*

What if you're in a hurry? Or if there's an emergency?

At times, many of us have opted to take a safety-look and then proceed through the intersection.

Sometimes in life, we have to do the same thing. If the past is always on red, let go of it and proceed.

Main point: Share this video clip of two veterans writing a song and letting go of the past in order to move forward..

Notice that, sometimes, we're letting go of good things in the past in order to make a transition.

Page: Not in workbook

Talking points: After the clip is over ask, *Can you relate to what these warriors said about transitions?*

Follow up with, *Have you seen this in your life— or in the life of another warrior— in good and bad ways?*

Quick tip: We cover five points related to walking into your potential:

1. Face the past— You can't move forward if you're still fighting yesterdays' battles; let it go (chapter 7)

2. Forgive yourself— Moral Injury (chapter 3)

3. Find your battle buddies— Don't travel alone; get in a web (chapter 6)

4. Fight for the present— Fight for a new mission / purpose, which includes:

   • Your family

   • Your fellow warriors

   • Your future

5. Forge ahead— (this will lead us to discussing the next mission, and right into the following chapter)

Main point: We're about to walk through 5 points related to moving fully into the present, which empowers us to walk in our potential. The first point is to face the past.

Page: 159

Talking point: Like J.T. and Matt say in the video, "You can't move forward if you're still fighting yesterday's battles."

We discussed this in chapter 7.

Main point: Remind warriors to deal with any feelings of guilt or shame they feel, as we outlined in chapter 3.

Page: 159

Talking point: The second point about living to your potential is to forgive yourself. You'll never walk in the boldness and authority you carry if you feel intimidated by your past.

Steps to Reach Potential

* FACE THE PAST
* FORGIVE YOURSELF
* FIND YOUR BATTLE BUDDIES

PAGE 159

Main point: The third point is to find battle buddies-- people to walk through life with.

Page: 159

Steps to Reach Potential

* FACE THE PAST
* FORGIVE YOURSELF
* FIND YOUR BATTLE BUDDIES
  DON'T TRAVEL ALONE-
  GET IN A WEB-
  CHAPTER 6

PAGE 159

Talking point: Remind warriors that in the same way they wouldn't go into battle alone, they shouldn't journey through life alone.

Refer them back to chapter 6, as well as to the concept of the "web" we mentioned in the introduction (see pages 13-14).

When you serve you are part of a "band of brothers," a web you might say. Encourage warriors to find that web today to help them through the battles of life.

Steps to Reach Potential

* FACE THE PAST
* FORGIVE YOURSELF
* FIND YOUR BATTLE BUDDIES
* FIGHT FOR THE PRESENT

PAGE 159

Main point: The fourth point is to actually fight for the present— with intensity and intention.

Page: 159

Steps to Reach Potential

* FACE THE PAST
* FORGIVE YOURSELF
* FIND YOUR BATTLE BUDDIES
* FIGHT FOR THE PRESENT
   FIGHT FOR A NEW
   MISSION / PURPOSE

PAGE 159

Talking point: Warriors should view the most important aspects of their lives with the same intensity and priority they viewed their past missions.

If you're having trouble giving that degree of focus and attention to these priorities, keep in mind that they need high level commitment. Remind them how important a life mission is— so fight for it.

THE PRESENT

A. YOUR FAMILY
B. YOUR FELLOW WARRIORS
C. YOUR FUTURE

PAGE 156

Main point: Three items should be on the "mission" list of each warrior:

A. Family (they cannot be excluded from the process of healing and defining the next mission)

B. Fellow Warriors (others who are on or have been on a similar journey)

C. Future (the action steps they must take today so that their planned future becomes a reality)

Page: 156

Steps to Reach Potential

* FACE THE PAST
* FORGIVE YOURSELF
* FIND YOUR BATTLE BUDDIES
* FIGHT FOR THE PRESENT
* FORGE AHEAD

PAGE 159

Main point: Fifth, finally, remind warriors to forge ahead.

Page: 159

Talking points: This leads us into the next slide about where the mission is...

MISSION
YOUR MISSION IS AHEAD OF YOU– NOT BEHIND YOU!

PAGE 163

Main point: The mission is ahead of us, not behind us.

Page: 163

Talking points: Remind the warriors that no matter how great the missions were which they have completed, they are all in the past.

We honor those past missions and remember them, but it is now time to move forward to the missions still before us— the ones which have not yet been accomplished.

Main point: This slide will lead us into the next chapter, talking about the future.

Page: 175

Talking point: Our "future us" is our "present us" or "current us" plus the steps we take each day. So, it's important that we learn to live fully present in the moment.

Main point: Dr. Luann Bourne is a Psychologist and well understands the affect combat can have on a warrior. She knows this not only because she is an expert in the field but also because her son served in the Middle East. This is her story about how her son's experience in combat affected him and her entire family.

Page: Her story is found on page 110.

9. EMBRACING THE FUTURE

YOUR OBJECTIVE: SHOW WARRIORS THAT THE PERSON THEY WILL BECOME IN THE FUTURE IS THE SAME PERSON THEY ARE NOW, WITH THE ADDITION OF THE STEPS THEY TAKE. ENCOURAGE THEM TO TAKE INTENTIONAL STEPS IN A PLANNED DIRECTION.

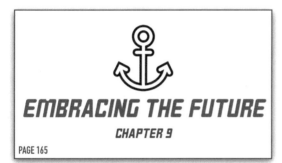

Main point: Title slide for chapter 9

Page: 165

Quick tip: We often live with a disconnect between who we are now and who we are in the future. We all want a better future, but we forget that our future begins now — and is the result of the steps we take each day in order to get there.

This disconnect is why so few people plan for retirement, don't monitor their health better in their younger days, etc.

When we give positive attention to our present, we also give positive attention to our future.

"THE BEST THING ABOUT THE FUTURE IS THAT IT COMES ONE DAY AT A TIME."

+ ABRAHAM LINCOLN

PAGE 164

Main point: The future doesn't have to be overwhelming. Regardless of how far we have to go to reach our destination or how much we need to achieve, we get to do it in bite-sized chunks.

When we try to do it all at once we can become overwhelmed and may drift back to the "failures" of the past.

Page: 164

Talking points: Ask the group if have ever been overwhelmed by the size of a mission or project.

If so, ask if they completed it.

Ask: *How were you able to finish it?*

If they didn't finish, ask what hindered it's completion.

Expect mixed responses. Some probably made a plan. Some probably ""suffered through it" and just did what had to be done, etc. Remind them that "quick fixes" rarely— if ever— work. We have to be in it for the long haul and be intentional.

MAIN IDEA

9. EMBRACING THE FUTURE

YOUR FUTURE BEGINS IN YOUR PRESENT. DO NOT SIT BACK AND SIMPLY WAIT FOR YOUR FUTURE TO UNFOLD - PLAN FOR IT - PLOT OUT YOUR MISSION. ACT ON THE PLAN AND MAKE ADJUSTMENTS AS NEEDED.

PAGE 165

Main point: Read the main idea

Page: 165

Talking points: Remind them that although we tend to think of the "future" as a distant reality, it begins now. We create our future with each new day, one day at a time.

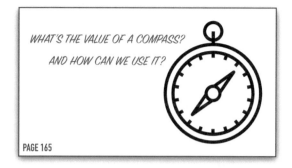

Main point: To get to our destination it is important to travel in the right direction.

Page: 164

Talking points: Ask, *What's the purpose of a compass?*

A compass plots direction. It doesn't give you every detail about what you'll face along the way, but it helps you chart your direction and stay on course.

Main point: When traveling, destination and direction are important.

Page: 166

Talking points: Point out the slide pictures two seemingly contradictory points of direction and destination:

- Left side: if you know where you want to go (destination) that determines the direction you should head.

- Right side: if you move in any direction— even without a plan— the direction you choose will determine where you end up.

Ask, *Which statement is true?*

Turns out, both are but only the left assures of getting us where we want to be.

Whether we make a plan or not, our actions determine where we end up in the future (right side). So, it's better to decide where we want to be (left side) and begin moving in that direction.

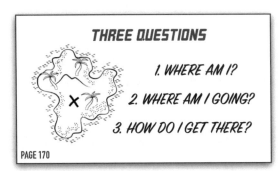

THREE QUESTIONS

1. WHERE AM I?

2. WHERE AM I GOING?

3. HOW DO I GET THERE?

PAGE 170

Main point: There are three things we need in order to go anywhere.

1. We must be honest about where we are.

2. We must decide where we want to be.

3. We need to make a plan to get there.

Page: 170

Talking points: Remind warriors that they might simultaneously work on multiple missions at the same time.

And they may be in a different "place" in each of them. For instance, they may be in excellent health, but have a failing marriage. Or they might be in great financial health, but lack purpose.

They can work on multiple missions concurrently. However, common to every mission is that we must have a plan. (Even the decision not to have a plan is a plan. It's not a very good one, but it's still a plan which takes you to a predictable destination.)

"HOW DO YOU EAT AN ELEPHANT?"
PAGE 171

Main point: It is not enough to complete the previous three steps. We must take action. However, it's better to take a little bit of consistent action every day rather than trying to "storm the castle" and do everything at once.

Page: 171

Talking points: The answer to this question is "one bite at a time."

Generate some discussion about this. Ask the group if they can think of some examples of trying to "eat the entire elephant" at once rather than bite-sized chunks.

Some examples include:

- Weight loss

- Finances and savings (consistency vs. a "get rich scheme" or even gambling)

- Learning a new trade or skill

- The "couch potato to 5-K" or any other exercise program

If you had to eat an elephant in one bite, you are destined for failure. However, give yourself enough time to take bite-sized chunks (and call in some battle buddies to help you), and you are much more likely to succeed.

LIVE FORWARD

THE PAST JUST EXPLAINS YOU.
IT DOESN'T DEFINE YOU.

PAGE 168

Main point: Two chapters ago we reminded warriors that we need to deal with the past, but we don't need to live there. When we drive a vehicle, we have a massive windshield to see what is ahead and tiny mirrors to see what is behind. This is a great metaphor for life.

Page: 168

Talking point: Ask, *When driving is most of your attention focused on the road ahead of you or the road you have already traveled?*

The answer is "the road ahead."

Yet, we still have rear view mirrors. We have them because in order to successfully navigate the road ahead of us we still need to know what is coming from behind.

In life our past often "sneaks up" on us and can impact our forward movement if we aren't aware of it. So, keep an eye on the past but focus your attention on the present and what is ahead.

Main point: We often want to grade our personal worth on where we find ourselves in life.

Page: 174

Talking points: Point out that if things are going well, we tend to feel valuable. If they're not, we often feel worthless. But where we find ourselves is simply our location— nothing more.

Where we find ourselves in life often (wrongly) dictates how we feel about ourselves.

Despite the circumstances of life, we can still be true to who we are, our mission, and those who travel with us.

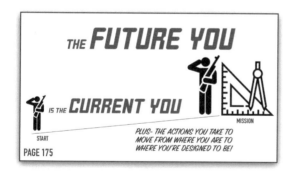

Main point: This is a similar slide to the one on pages 97-98, where we discussed the "gap" and the "gain" and the "messy middle." You may want to refer back to the previous lesson (chapter 5, Overcoming Obstacles) and show the group how these concepts all fit together.

Page: 175

Talking point: Just as the past you determined who you are in the present, the present you is shaping who you will be in the future. By taking care of the present you, you are also taking care of the future you.

Main point: Dr. Elspeth Ritchie was a Colonel in the army and has served as Chief Clinical Officer for the Department of Mental Health. She understands how and why so many veterans are still dealing with the past. That said, she also reminds us of the tremendous abilities veterans have to offer based on their training and time in the service.

Page: Her story is found on page 176.

10. FACING FORWARD

YOUR OBJECTIVE: REMIND WARRIORS THAT THE SKILL SET TRANSFERRED TO THEM AND THE MINDSET INSTILLED IN THEM DURING THEIR TRAINING STILL WORKS IN THEIR LIVES OUTSIDE OF MILITARY SERVICE.

Main point: Title slide for chapter 10

Page: 181

Quick tip: The purpose of Unit 4 (Empowerment = E), chapter 10, is simple: give the warriors an opportunity to reminisce about the high points of their service — including the boot camp they graduated, and remind them that their training — which is some of the best, most all-encompassing in the world — still works.

They retain the skills and the mindset needed to thrive as a warrior, and that training will work just as successfully in other areas of life.

> "LEADERS BECOME GREAT, NOT BECAUSE OF THEIR POWER, BUT BECAUSE OF THEIR ABILITY TO EMPOWER OTHERS."
> *JOHN MAXWELL*
>
>
>
> PAGE 180

Main point: Read the quote and remind the warriors that we learned that partnering with others is essential to our mission (chapter 6).

Page: 180

Talking points: This quote leads into the main idea of the chapter, the next slide.

MAIN IDEA

10. FACING FORWARD

PAGE 181

YOU STILL HAVE MUCH TO OFFER IN SERVICE TO OTHERS. THE MISSION IS BEFORE YOU. EMBRACE IT AND EMPOWER OTHERS.

Main point: Warriors are invaluable in today's society. They need to be included.

Page: 181

Talking points: Emphasize each part of the main idea:

- They still have a lot to offer— the best days don't have to be behind them.

- Any mission they have from this point on is in front of them-- not behind.

- Empowering others is an important part of moving forward, as it will provide an ongoing mission.

Quick tip: Boot camp is something every warrior— regardless of the branch of military in which they served— has in common. They will all remember high points, humorous episodes, and "war stories" about how difficult boot camp was.

We cannot emphasize enough to give them the opportunity to share. This is a non-threatening topic, but has profound lessons when applied.

BOOT CAMP

PAGE 181

Main point: Boot camp is an important marker in the life of a warrior.

Page: 181

Talking points: Generate discussion on this topic.

Ask the group, *Who remembers boot camp?*

Then ask, *What was boot camp like for you? What memories do you have?*

Ask, *Was bootcamp important? If so, why?*

Note: make sure to provide enough time for everyone who wants to speak to have the opportunity to do so. Whereas some participants choose not to respond aloud to some of the more reflective questions we ask, many will readily jump into this conversation.

Main point: Bootcamp serves many purposes. But there are three objectives that carry forward into life outside of service.

Page: 182

Talking points: Ask the warriors if the objectives on this slide accurately reflect what was instilled in them.

(Notice, this slide shifts the conversation to a more serious tone.)

Point out, *Not all of your training has application outside of service. For example, one warrior who was trained as a sniper, said, "That particular skill set doesn't transfer well to the general public."*

Then, conclude, *However, the three objectives listed here are still part of you and will help carry you forward in life.*

Main point: This is a video of J.T. Cooper reciting the Soldier's Creed which he learned as part of his training.

Page: J.T.'s quote is found on page 182.

Talking points: Ask the group if they can relate, and if anyone would like to share their thoughts.

HEALING

* MENTAL
* EMOTIONAL
* SPIRITUAL

OPPORTUNITY

* DEFINE THE MISSION
* OVERCOME OBSTACLES
* PARTNER WITH OTHERS

PEACE

* FACE THE PAST
* OWN THE PRESENT
* EMBRACE THE FUTURE

Main point: The next few slides are a review of where we've been for the previous 10 lessons (intro week + 9 chapters).

Page: Slides not in workbook.

You may choose to refer to the Table of Contents on pages 5-6 to show them.

Talking points: Take your time and provide them with an overview.

1. We've discussed healing, which may be an ongoing process— particularly as we seek health in every area of life.

2. We've talked about finding a new mission— and decided that we should expect to face a few obstacles on the way, which is one of the reasons we want to partner with others.

3. We've come to terms with the past and have committed to live fully present "now" while having a future orientation.

Main point: Show the slide and ask them, *Who is closer to reaching their goal?*

Page: Slide not in workbook.

Talking points: Everyone will assess this correctly- that the man on the bottom is technically closer, but he won't succeed because he has stopped moving forward. The failure only comes when you cease moving.

The man on the top has the greatest potential to succeed. Don't ever stop short of your objective.

This leads us to the slide for this lesson....

Main point: We want to— like the man on the top— continue chipping away at our mission as we move forward. Even if it seems like we have a long way to go.

Page: Slide not in workbook.

Talking points: The man who quit on the previous slide probably had no idea how close he was— he just got tired of trying or got discouraged and gave up. It's easy to do.

Remember, it's easier to continue if we have people walking with us, people who remind us of the mission and our part in it. That's why we need to be part of a team.

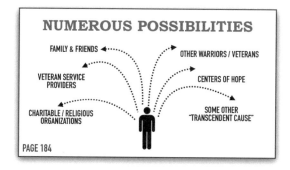

Main point: There are numerous possibilities for a mission in life.

Page: 184

Talking points: Remind warriors that these are only a few suggestions. We've seen warriors "take on" their grandkids as a mission, serving through a nonprofit or other group, or even creating a new venture.

Be sure and stress a great mission would be to find warriors who need help or a mission and bring them to the next Center of Hope.

Quick tip: Perhaps you know of some specific needs in your area. If you're leading this group at a church, community center, or other organization, you may be able to direct warriors to a particular service this organization needs. Feel free to provide real examples and opportunities to the group.

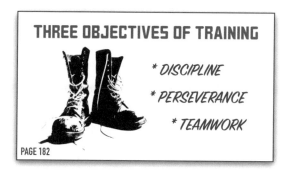

Main point: Remind warriors that these are the objectives of boot camp — and we discussed how each of these were instilled in each of them.

Page: 182

Talking points: Point out that these are still part of them, and these traits prove helpful in *every* life mission.

Main point: The training still works.

Page: 186

Talking points: Warriors are given some of the deepest, most-immersive, all-encompassing training.

Remind them not to forget this and that it works in every area of life.

Point out that warriors are trained to succeed in both service and in life. They still have great value.

Main point: Ask the group if their time in Centers of Hope helped. If so, we would love to hear from them. Our contact info is provided in the book.

Page: 187

Talking points: We are always interested in finding leaders and co-leaders for future centers, as well. Invite them to join this movement if they are interested in making Centers of Hope part of their next mission.

Main point: As you dismiss the group, remind the warriors of who they are. If you plan on having a celebration session, be sure and announce it.

Page: 195

Talking point: The following page provides you with three options on how to conclude your group.

OPTION 1

Let this be the last meeting and let members know when the next group will start so they can recruit others to attend. If you have not yet set a start date for the next group, let them know you will email that information to them as soon as it has been determined.

OPTION 2

Let this be the last meeting but give members a challenge coin. Will be the same as option one except it includes providing members with a Challenge Coin. The Challenge Coin is a powerful reminder of what they have accomplished and of their experience together.

How you handle giving out the coins can be personal to each group. Here are some suggestions.

1. Have each member come to the front and you give them the coin. You may want to say something personal about each person to encourage them to continue their journey.

2. Another suggestion is to go to each member in their seat and give them their coin. Again, you may want to add a personal word of encouragement to each as you give them their coin.

3. If you have a large group, you may need to simply pass the coins out at one time due to time constraints.

Whichever method you choose be sure to include the following information during the coin ceremony.

Point out the coin has been designed to remind them of their accomplishments and to be on mission. On one side is the Centers of Hope logo with the reminder to always:

- Seek healing – mental, emotional, and spiritual

- Find opportunities to connect with others

- Receive the peace that is theirs, and that

- They are empowered to live a new mission

Point out that on the other side of the coin is the Warriors on Mission logo to remind them that the actions they take now are building a legacy of service to others that they too might find HOPE.

Be sure and challenge them once more to be part of the next group and to bring a buddy.

OPTION 3

Have a follow up celebration meeting with or without an inexpensive meal. (If having a meal, perhaps your hosting organization will send representatives and provide it.)

If having a celebration meeting/meal be sure and announce the time and place if different from your regular meeting place. This could even be done in an inexpensive restaurant.

Use this time to allow members to share what they thought of their experience with Centers of Hope. Find out if there is anything else they felt that should have been covered or that they would like to have spent more time on.

If you intend on providing a Challenge Coin, be sure and allow enough time to incorporate Option 2 into the meeting.

Be sure and let them know when the next group will start or tell them you will email that information to them.

ABOUT THE AUTHORS

Bob Waldrep has been engaged in cultural apologetics, with an emphasis on new religious movements, since 1993. Through the years, he has observed and addressed cultural trends that have altered various elements of our society; especially, as pertains to matters of faith and spirituality. In early 2008, he founded the Crosswinds Foundation to be a resource for those individuals and organizations being impacted by new and different emerging cultural trends. Waldrep is the co-writer and Executive Producer for the films, *Invisible Scars*, which addresses the trauma associated with PTSD, and *Honoring the Code*, which deals with Moral Injury. In addition to these documentaries, he coauthored *The Truth Behind the Secret* (Harvest House); is a contributor to *The Popular Encyclopedia of Apologetics* (Harvest House) and *The Complete Evangelism Guidebook* (Baker Books); and scripted the documentary *The Da Vinci Code Revealed*. He has appeared as an expert commentator for print, radio, television and Internet media, locally, nationally and internationally; including appearances on: ABC's World News Tonight; ABC's Night Line; MSNBC with Brian Williams; CNN; NHK-TV, Tokyo; USA Today; Time; Newsweek; and Christianity Today.

Bob's father served in the 88th Infantry Division during WWII and, after researching and producing the *Invisible Scars* film, Bob said, "I found myself reevaluating my own familial experience. Through the process I realized my own father suffered with PTSD. His experiences in WWII had clearly left their own scars. But, the truth is they weren't exactly invisible. They could be seen in the nightmares that plagued his sleep, in the attitude with which he faced the world, and in the alcohol which offered temporary relief. I am convinced his life would have been different if someone could have shared something like *Invisible Scars* with him."

Waldrep has been researching the emotional and mental traumas associated with military service since 2012. Since that time he has spoken with and interviewed hundreds of veterans and experts in the field of trauma. This research and these relationships form the foundation for *Warrior Hope*.

Andrew Edwin Jenkins oversees the Centers of Hope effort for Crosswinds.

He has been speaking and writing for almost two decades— in some shape or form. He's served as a fundraiser for the Salvation Army, has served on staff at multiple churches, and has worked at several nonprofits helping men, women, and families coming off the streets, away from addictions, the prison system, and human trafficking.

Andrew launched a health and wellness business a few years ago, enabling him to work from home. Now, he writes and teaches full-time— in person and online.

He empowers people to live healthy in every area of their life— physically, emotionally, and spiritually- so they can reach their full potential and live their true destiny.

He's written over a dozen books (including *Redemption*, *The Emotional Wholeness Checklist*, *The Next Best Step*, and *Advance*), speaks at live events, and hosts a weekly podcast.

Learn more at www.Jenkins.tv.

Made in the USA
Columbia, SC
10 February 2024

31205448R00085